T0339458

The Resilient School Leader

Learn practical ways to manage the stress of being a school leader so you can get the most out of your career. In this follow up to the bestseller *17 Things Resilient Teachers Do (and Four Things They Hardly Ever Do)*, Bryan Harris and Janet Gilbert present strategies to help school leaders build resilience on a daily basis. Topics covered include focusing on purpose, prioritizing relationships, protecting your time, refining communication, being mindful and self-aware, recognizing and combatting burnout, taking risks, forgiving and apologizing, understanding change, and having fun. Each of the 20 short chapters presents a concise summary of the topic, a deeper look at what it means, and a list of practical applications that you can implement right away. With this guidebook, you'll feel ready to bounce back from challenges and stay focused on the many rewards of leadership.

Bryan Harris has been an educator for more than 30 years. Starting as a middle school teacher and serving in roles such as elementary school principal, central office administrator, and trainer/consultant, he now serves as an Associate Professor of Education at Arizona Christian University.

Janet Gilbert has had the privilege of serving students and staff in a school setting from preschool to 8th grades. She loves teaching adults and has worked as an adjunct instructor at Phoenix College for 15 years.

The Resilient School Leader

20 Ways to Manage Stress and Build Resilience

Bryan Harris and Janet Gilbert

Routledge
Taylor & Francis Group

NEW YORK AND LONDON

Designed cover image: © Getty Images

First published 2023
by Routledge
605 Third Avenue, New York, NY 10158

and by Routledge
4 Park Square, Milton Park, Abingdon, Oxon, OX14 4RN

Routledge is an imprint of the Taylor & Francis Group, an informa business

© 2023 Bryan Harris and Janet Gilbert

The right of Bryan Harris and Janet Gilbert to be identified as authors of this work has been asserted in accordance with sections 77 and 78 of the Copyright, Designs and Patents Act 1988.

Library of Congress Cataloging-in-Publication Data
Names: Harris, Bryan (Teacher) author. | Gilbert, Janet, author.
Title: The resilient school leader : 20 ways to manage stress and build resilience / Bryan Harris and Janet Gilbert.
Description: New York, NY : Routledge, 2023. |
Includes bibliographical references. |
Identifiers: LCCN 2022049189 | ISBN 9781032293769 (hardback) |
ISBN 9781032278438 (paperback) | ISBN 9781003301356 (ebook)
Subjects: LCSH: Educational leadership–Psychological aspects. |
Educators–Job stress. | Educators–Professional relationships. |
Resilience (Personality trait) | Burn out (Psychology)–Prevention.
Classification: LCC LB2806 .H345 2023 |
DDC 371.2/011–dc23/eng/20221220
LC record available at https://lccn.loc.gov/2022049189

ISBN: 978-1-032-29376-9 (hbk)
ISBN: 978-1-032-27843-8 (pbk)
ISBN: 978-1-003-30135-6 (ebk)

DOI: 10.4324/9781003301356

Typeset in Palatino
by Newgen Publishing UK

To educational leaders everywhere. Thanks for what you do.

Contents

About the Authors

Dr. Bryan Harris has been an educator for more than 30 years. Starting as a middle school teacher and serving in roles such as elementary school principal, central office administrator, and trainer/consultant, he now serves as an Associate Professor of Education at Arizona Christian University. For more information about Dr. Harris, his other books, or to contact him for training opportunities go to www.bryan-harris.com.

Dr. Janet Gilbert has had the privilege of serving students and staff in a school setting from preschool to 8th grades. Her passion for improving teaching and learning has developed throughout her 25 years in education. She has been a general education teacher, special education teacher, reading specialist, instructional coach, and administrator. She holds four degrees with the most recent being a Ph.D. in general psychology with emphasis in cognition and instruction from Grand Canyon University. She loves teaching adults and has worked as an adjunct instructor at Phoenix College for 15 years. For more information about Dr. Gilbert go to https://janetgilbert.consulting.

Acknowledgements, Gratitude, and Appreciations

Writing a book is hard work. It takes focus, effort, motivation, overcoming obstacles, and meeting (and sometimes not meeting) deadlines and expectations. It takes, surprise – a decent amount of resilience.

But most importantly, writing a book takes teamwork and collaboration.

We owe a debt of gratitude and immense appreciation to many people for their support, encouragement, and assistance in making this book a reality.

- ♦ To our spouses, children, and families – We are blessed and thankful that God has put us together.
- ♦ To a network of passionate and dedicated educators who helped us along our journey – we are blessed to be connected with LaVonna Roth, LeAnn Nickelsen, Shauna King, Linnea Lyding, Kimberly Alexander, Jessica Tucker, and the greater network of colleagues and friends in the Deer Valley Unified School District in Arizona and the team at Arizona Christian University.
- ♦ To our editor, Lauren Davis, and the team at Routledge – Thanks for believing in us and offering support, encouragement, and insight.

Introduction

Since no one likes to read long introductions, let's get right to the point.

When *17 Things Resilient Teachers Do (and 4 Things They Hardly Ever Do)* was released in 2020, there was an almost immediate request for a leadership edition ... something like *17 Things Resilient School Leaders Do*. My (Bryan speaking here) initial response was something akin to "Well, you could just take any place you see the word "teacher" and replace it with whatever title you want – "principal," "director," "superintendent." The concepts work regardless of the title one wears on a daily basis.

But being a school leader is a unique and challenging thing. The more I thought about (and the more feedback I got), the more I became convinced that a leadership edition would be a good thing. So here we are.

In case you've not had a chance to read *17 Things Resilient Teachers Do* (which would be a shame, by the way – it's really good), here are the premises that book and this book are built upon:

♦ **Stress, as we'll define it, focuses on control**. In short, when we perceive that something (a situation, a context, a relationship, an event) is beyond our control, our stress response kicks in. If you like to highlight things and annotate in the margins of books, write this, "Stress is all about control." A more concrete definition of stress is this: It is the brain/body response to a perception of a lack of control over an adverse situation (Jensen, 2005). When we are in a situation where we perceive that we have little or no control, the brain is designed to respond by providing the resources to gain back some sense of control. What are those resources, you ask? Primarily cortisol and adrenaline. Quite simply, those resources are designed to give you the attentional focus, physical energy, and problem-solving skills to figure out how to gain back some control. If stress is the brain/body response to a perception of a lack of control, then where do we start? You've already guessed it; we start by getting some control. When we gain control of our thinking patterns, physical movement, the words we speak, etc., our stress levels go down. Stress and control are inversely related. After all, if you have control over something, it's probably not stressing you out.

♦ **Short-term stress is healthy. Long-term stress is deadly.** You can't avoid stress. Why? Because you can't control everything around you. Nor do you want to try to avoid stress. In the short term, those brain resources (cortisol and adrenaline plus some others), are great. In the short term, they help with attention, problem solving, memory, and they equip you with physical energy (Sapolsky, 2004). Those all sound good, right? That's because they are. The problem, as you've guessed by now, is when cortisol and adrenaline stick around for too long. When they spend too much time in your system, when they don't have a chance to dissipate as they are designed, we experience distress or chronic stress. When stress levels stay high for too long, bad things happen to our brains, our bodies, our mental health, and our relationships.

♦ **Stress is really about the *perception* of control.** We just stated that "stress is about control." While that's true, it's a bit more nuanced than that. It's really about the perception of how much control we have at any given moment (Levitin, 2020). It's really about the belief we have about how much control we have over that adverse situation. Without going into a long-winded detour about why this is, suffice it to say that it's about survival. Our brains are designed to keep us alive; survival is your brain's primary purpose. Your system (when we refer to the "system," we are referring to the brain and body) is designed to respond to things that might be a threat to your survival. Some threats are real, some are perceived. The response from your system is the same regardless. Whether the threat is real or just perceived (not real), cortisol and adrenaline are released and your system gets ready to deal with the threat/stressor. This is actually great news. Why? When we change or adjust the ways we perceive things, we can manage that stressor better. We'll do a deeper dive into this in coming chapters but think about it this way – if we choose to perceive or think about a challenging situation differently (use the word "opportunity" instead of "challenge," for example), we're taking control. When we have some sense of control, our stress levels go down.

◆ **While ubiquitous in our profession, stress can be managed.** The goal is not to eliminate stress (which cannot be done anyway); the goal is to practice effective ways to manage the stress we do experience. The good news is that this entire book is all about managing those stressors.

◆ **The way to manage stress is by building, practicing, and refining personal resilience.** This will be a lifelong journey, by the way. But we start with small steps and build momentum. That momentum then builds into habits and those habits build a better life. It's also important to note that resilience isn't a mountain to conquer. You'll probably not get to a point in life where you proclaim, "I am 100% resilient! I am at the top of the mountain." It's a process and a set of skills that develop and build over time. And, resilience is really not one singular thing. It's a set of skills, habits, and beliefs, that we put into practice in order to manage stress.

◆ **Resilience, as we'll define it, consists of two things: how we think and what we do.** Resilience, in the literature and research, is most commonly referred to as an individual's ability to cope with challenging situations. You'll often see resilience as analogous to a bouncing ball (we "bounce back" after a setback), a ship navigating difficult waters (finding the best path through a difficult time), or even like life's shock absorbers (like the shocks and springs on your car, they influence how you experience the road but they don't actually *change* the road). Throughout this book, we'll offer specific strategies and techniques to practice and refine personal resilience. Some of those strategies focus on how we think (mindsets, thinking patterns, self-talk, etc.); other strategies focus on what we do (external coping mechanisms to employ during times of stress). If you are looking for a short, to-the-point, and (in our opinion) accurate definition of resilience as it relates specifically to being a school leader, we'll adopt Patterson and Kelleher's (2005) definition – *using your energy productively to emerge from adversity stronger than eve*r.

What we've attempted to do in this book is assemble the strategies, techniques, and practices that are effective at managing stress and building resilience. We've looked at the research – we'll share some of that along the way. We've considered our own practices and habits based on that research – and we've put these ideas into practice in our own lives. We'll offer concrete, effective strategies that work to manage stress and build resilience. And we'll point you in the right direction to further your own learning. Essentially, this book combines the best of what the research evidence says with common sense, practical applications. We are attempting to answer (at least partially) the question, "In the face of all the challenges we experience as school leaders, what can we do?"

Being a school leader is stressful. But that's not a news flash. You already know that. The real issue isn't so much the stress you experience; *the real issue is how you deal with the stress you have.* You can't get rid of stress. Nor should you want to. Stress is not a bad thing. Your system (the brain, the body) was designed to deal with stress. Stress is not the enemy. In fact, you need stress to function properly. The real enemy is long-term, unchecked, undealt-with stress. Throughout this book we'll provide ways to help you put that stress in check. We'll show you where to start and how to have a healthy relationship with stress by practicing resilience.

So let's jump in. You'll be glad you did.

Four Ways to Get the Most Out of This Book

1. View each of the broad categories (the 20 chapters) and the hundreds of Application Points as guidelines, not rules. Rules, by nature and definition, remove control. Remember that stress and control are inversely related. When you have little control, your stress goes up. But when you have control, choice, and voice, it's much easier to manage stress. What we provide here are guidelines, based on best practices, that are empowering, effective, and (perhaps most importantly) practical and do-able.

2. Remember the difference between simple and easy. The ideas we outline in this book are simple … the concepts, the Application Points, the take home messages … all straightforward and uncomplicated. But just because something is simple, does not mean it is easy. Becoming more resilient will take work. It will require effort and it will require that you be honest with yourself and do a decent amount of self-reflection. You'll learn to be more resilient the same way you learn anything – practice, trial and error, feedback, success, and reflection.

3. Share, talk, discuss – If you find these ideas powerful, don't keep them to yourself. Influence as many people as you can. Maybe start your own blog, lead a book study, research ideas for your own book, or give a presentation at a conference. Whatever you do, in big ways or small, you'll find that your resilience increases as you share these ideas with others.

4. Question, read, research, and learn – Don't just take our word for things, do your own investigation and learn from leading thinkers in the field. Read the work of noted researchers like Werner and Smith (The Kauai Study), Martin Seligman (the guy who taught us about the power of positive psychology), Nan Henderson and Mike

Milstein (and their popular Resiliency Wheel model), Norman Garmezy, Steven and Sybil Wolin, Bonnie Benard, Rick Hanson, Daniel Goleman, and more recently the work of Elena Aguilar (*Onward: Cultivating Emotional Resilience in Educators*, 2018). Look into the work of The Greater Good Science Center from the University of California at Berkeley or The Search Institute based out of Minnesota, both of which have great websites full of free resources. We've certainly missed some important people and organizations doing great work. For that, we apologize. The point is that there are some wonderful people doing important work and we look to them to continue refining our own understanding of resilience.

1

Resilient School Leaders – Put Their Masks on First

In a Nutshell ✅

Resilient school leaders understand that taking care of their health is job #1. When we take care of ourselves – when we attend to our own needs – the very best of us can be on display and we can be ready to support those around us. We start by taking care of our physical health.

Digging Deeper 🔍

Recall the last time you were on an airplane. As part of the pre-flight safety talk, a flight attendant said something like, "In the event of a loss in cabin pressure, oxygen masks will fall from the ceiling. Place your masks on first before attempting to help anyone else." When I first thought about this directive, I thought it a bit strange. If, for example, I'm traveling with a young child, I'm going to make sure that child is safe before I worry about myself. But there's a problem with this approach – if you have passed out or are unconscious, there is no way you can

DOI: 10.4324/9781003301356-1

help anyone else. The essence of "putting your mask on first" is making sure that you are healthy enough to take care of the people you lead.

You've likely heard people refer to "self-care" and the import-ance of making time to attend to your personal needs. In essence, this chapter is a reminder of the need to take care of yourself. While we are not necessarily fans of the term "self-care" (at least the way it's used in popular culture), the idea centers on the fact that you need to make yourself at least as important as you make others.

If you're not familiar with the concept of self-care (or putting your mask on first), a good definition comes from Shari Betts in her 2022 book *The ABCs of Self-Care*; it is "making deliberate choices to protect our mental, emotional, and physical health." She goes on to say that health care is "floss for the soul." As your dentist has likely said – you don't need to floss all your teeth, only the ones you want to keep. The same goes with taking care of yourself. Attend to those areas of your life that are important – specifically your physical health – so that you can help others secure their "masks" in the event of a loss in life's cabin pressure.

One more note about "self-care" – one of the reasons we are not big fans of the term is that it implies specific activities (such as meditation or yoga) or assumes that it takes place in a certain location (like a day spa). Plus, the research-base supporting self-care is founded in stress management and resilience; so we prefer to stick with solid evidence. And, if you do a quick internet search, you'll see that we are not alone. In fact, in 2020 *Psychology Today* published an article titled "Self-Care is Nonsense." While we won't go that far, the key thing to remember is that taking care of yourself (in whatever ways are most effective for you) is what will help to build your resili-ence. Quite simply, there is no one best way to practice self-care. Listed below in the Application Points, we'll offer lots of options to choose from.

Before we get to the specific strategies and techniques, it may be helpful to offer a few quick reminders about the connection between physical health and resilience:

◆ Your body is a system. To the brain, there is no separate thing called the body and to the body there is no separate thing called the brain. The brain and body are designed to work together in harmony. Whatever has an impact on the body also has an impact on the brain.

◆ Movement is a natural anti-depressant (Mayo Clinic, 2017).

◆ Heart health (i.e. a "heart healthy diet") is brain health (Gardener, 2016).

◆ Regular exercise improves mental flexibility (Burzynska, et al., 2015).

◆ Poor quality sleep is a risk factor for anxiety, depression, and mental fatigue (Steiger & Pawlowski, 2019).

◆ Diet impacts mental health and stress levels (Bremner et al., 2020).

The "put your mask on first" analogy is common. But, in all honesty, it may not be the best metaphor for leadership. Why? In real life, the masks only come out when it's an emergency. You probably don't live your daily life as an emergency (or, if you do, that's an entirely different discussion). But the idea here is to take care of yourself regularly so that when there are emergencies, you are healthy and equipped to help those around you.

Rick Hanson, author of *Resilient: How to Grow an Unshakeable Core of Calm, Strength, and Happiness* (2018), reminds us that the Golden Rule is a two-way street. We should treat others *and* ourselves in respectful and affirming ways. Take care of others and take care of yourself. He asks, "If you think of yourself as someone to whom you have a duty of care and kindness, what might change in how you talk to yourself, and how you go about your day?"

One last note you may find interesting – in a talk to high school students, billionaire Warren Buffet once asked students to consider how they'd act if they could have any car they wanted. But there was a catch. The catch was that it would be the only car they'd ever own. Knowing that this one car would be the only car they'd ever have, that this one vehicle would have to last for their entire lifetime, he asked them to think about how they'd treat that car. How might they drive it differently? How might the maintenance and care of the car be different if it had to last 70+ years? With that in mind, he then reminded the students that we each get one body. And that body needs to last a lifetime.

Application Points

- ◆ *Avoid excuses* – Don't justify poor habits by claiming that you don't have the time or the money to adopt healthy habits. The truth is that we all make the time (and set aside the money) to do those things we value the most. On the flip side, if we should avoid excuses, we should also avoid guilt. Don't feel guilty for taking time to attend to your needs.

- ◆ *Rest and relax* – Remember to schedule time to relax and take a breath. We know school days are busy and hectic but it's important to occasionally slow down and take stock of the moment. Perhaps place some rest and relaxation time on our daily schedule. Do what Anna Barnes, in her wonderfully concise book *How to De-Stress* (2021) advises – find a "haven" – a location that allows you to relax. That, by the way, is probably not in your office! We know that it can be a challenge to turn off your brain because of the lengthy list of tasks you need to accomplish. Remember that *busy does not mean productive.* Being busy is not the goal. Nor is it the goal to necessarily get lots of stuff done. The goal is to do the right things that have the right impact. It's much easier to focus on the right things when we've had the necessary rest.

- ◆ *Sleep* – There are undoubtedly times during the school year when good, quality sleep is elusive. That's true of educators at every level. But remember that sleep is about restoration; sometimes referred to as the "brain's rinse cycle," it restores and rebalances the body and the mind. When you feel out of balance, overwhelmed, or rushed, the need for sleep is greatest. One last note – sleep deprivation is not an act of courage or a badge to wear proudly. Lacking sleep actually works against you because in the long run you'll make more mistakes, mess up more relationships, and miss important events. Sleep is a key to managing stress (Hirotsu, et al., 2015).

◆ *Drink water* – There is a direct link between dehydration and stress. In fact, a 2018 study found that those who drank more water experienced less anxiety and depression when compared to the general population (Haghighatdoost et al., 2018). And, dehydration can increase stress and stress can cause us to become dehydrated (Liska et al., 2019). That's a cycle we want to avoid. We're not physicians so seek advice from a trusted medical professional but a current recommendation for water consumption suggests that women should aim for about 11 cups per day and men should aim for about 15 (Zelman, 2008).

◆ *Refine your diet* – You may have heard the phrase that "food impacts mood." The connection between what we eat and how we feel (including our overall mental well-being is well established). Do a quick internet search for "foods that impact mood" for a list of healthy options. If you need more evidence, consider the 2022 study published in the *Journal of Physical Activity and Health* that found a direct connection between ultra-processed foods and severe mental health problems (Hecht, et al., 2022). Fast food is not only bad for your waistline, it's bad for your mental health as well.

◆ *Eat "foods that love you back"* – That's what Dr. Daniel Amen, author of *You, Happier* (2022) calls foods that have a direct impact on your emotional health. We know that what we eat impacts our ability to manage stress. So an easy place to begin is by adjusting the fuel that is put into the body. Dr. Amen also reminds us that "fast food is sad food" and highlights that what we eat and drink "has a direct effect" on our brains. A great place to find a list of foods that promote stress reduction is www.danielplan.com/eat-foods-that-love-you-back/.

◆ *Take care of your gut* – While we're on the subject of diet and "foods that boost your mood," it's important to note the connection between digestive health and brain health. Recall that the brain and body are connected – they work as a system. Within the last decade or so, scientists have discovered interesting (if not odd) connections between the brain and the gut. For example, it is estimated that 90% of our body's serotonin is produced in the digestive system (Yano et al., 2015). Taking care of your digestive system is a significant way to manage your emotional health.

◆ *Get outside* – Being in nature improves mental well-being. A 2020 article by the American Psychological Association titled "Nurtured by Nature" says it this way, "Spending time in nature can act as a 'balm for busy brains'." There is even a growing field of research called ecotherapy that uses time in nature and the outdoors to heal people from trauma.

◆ *Exercise* – The link between physical health and overall health (including cognition) is well established (Ohrnberger et al., 2017). When we move our bodies, our brains respond in positive ways. Most notably, it releases what we might describe as the brain's "happy" chemicals (dopamine and serotonin). In case you needed more convincing, there is mounting evidence that emotional well-being is highly influenced (if not outright driven) by physical health (Ghannoum et al., 2021).

◆ *Stretch and breathe* – When we feel stress, our whole body responds. Our breathing quickens, our muscles tense up, and our system prepares to battle the pending threat. This happens by design. When we breathe and stretch, it's a way for our bodies to mediate some of the tension.

◆ *Remember to say "no"* – This is a recommendation that you'll see several times throughout this book. In fact, in *17 Things Resilient Teachers Do* (2021), Bryan devoted an entire chapter to the topic. We won't recount that chapter here but suffice it to say that our stress levels are often directly related to how much we take on; at times we simply say yes to too many things. And if we are doing too many things, the first to go (for many of us) is our physical health.

◆ *Think selfishly* – Long before there was a discussion about self-care and stress management for educators, Todd Whitaker, along with Beth Whitaker and Dale Lumpa (2008), wrote that leaders need to think and act selfishly at times in order to be effective. Take time to take care of yourself, at don't apologize for it. You need outlets for personal renewal and health. Because, as you may have heard, "When the principal sneezes, the whole school catches a cold."

2

Resilient School Leaders – Count Their Blessings (Daily)

In a Nutshell ✓

One of the best ways to mitigate the negative effects of stress is to acknowledge the blessings and good fortune you've experienced in your life and career. Daily acts of gratitude, it turns out, are a wonderful way to buffer the daily stressors of leadership.

Digging Deeper

Discussions of gratitude can be found throughout history. Over the years, philosophers, teachers, theologians, and even scientists have studied gratitude and thankfulness. They've tackled questions related to religion, culture, cognition, and overall health. Questions led to more questions and some researchers have studied where gratitude comes from and why some people are more grateful than others.

In the early 2000s researchers started taking a hard look (and applying scientific research methods) to ask and answer questions about the benefits of gratitude. They've attempted

DOI: 10.4324/9781003301356-2

to define the concept within the context of mental and physical health outcomes.

Although it could mean different things to different people at different times, Dr. Robert Emmons, perhaps the world's leading researcher delving into the connection between gratitude and health, explained that gratitude has two essential elements: "recognizing that one has obtained a positive outcome" and "recognizing that there is an external source for this positive outcome" (Emmons & McCullough, 2003). Essentially, this means that gratitude is not just acknowledging the goodness around you, it's also taking the time to appreciate where that goodness comes from.

So why should be we be grateful? What are the emotional, physical, and relational benefits to practicing gratitude on a daily basis? How might it help us be better school leaders (and better people in general)?

In one of the deepest and most systematic academic reviews of the impact of gratitude, researchers from New Zealand (Boggiss et al., 2020) found that grateful people tend to be heathier, happier, and live longer. They also report that individuals who practiced gratitude reported feeling less stressed and less worried, which improved their emotional well-being and overall health. In addition, grateful people reported improved sleep, more patience, better relationships, and had an increase in satisfaction with work and school. Basically, affirming what is good in life has a positive impact in every aspect of our lives.

You may be wondering where gratitude comes from. Over the years, it has been suggested that gratitude is an intrinsic part of our DNA (Allen, 2018). In essence, it may be a part of our design and make up related to our species need to survive and get along with one another.

We know that being grateful and counting your daily blessings improves health. But, it also helps to build resiliency over time. In recent years, neurologists have looked to see how our brain reacts when we think about gratitude. They found that there was more activity in the prefrontal cortex, which suggested that gratitude was associated with life satisfaction (Kong et al.,

2020). It turns out that counting our blessings (daily) is good for the brain.

Ultimately, keep in mind that when we refer to resiliency, we mean two things: how we think and what we do. By practicing gratitude, you are building resiliency. Being grateful is an action; an action that must be purposeful and intentional. And when we are purposeful and intentional with those we lead, great things happen. Fishman (2020) reminds us that life offers numerous opportunities each day for gratitude towards others. Recognizing people for small things (offering a compliment, for example) amplifies positive emotions. The practice of gratitude becomes easier when we express them out loud. That becomes a win-win for both you and those you lead. As a school leader, model the practice of expressing gratitude and encourage others to do the same.

Application Points

- ◆ *Start now* – Today is the perfect day to get started. There is no need to wait for a special occasion. Look around and find something to be grateful for.
- ◆ *Practice reframing* – Reframing is a form of internal dialogue (self-talk) where we make an intentional effort to think differently about a situation confronting us. We start by being mindful of our own thinking patterns and the assumptions or biases that we may have unintentionally adopted. We then make an effort to view the situation from a different, more productive perspective. If you'd like to learn more about the art of reframing, an entire chapter was devoted to it in *17 Things Resilient Teachers Do (and 4 Things They Hardly Ever Do)* (Harris, 2021).
- ◆ *Write it down* – Writing is a great way to externalize thinking. Some leaders utilize a gratitude journal while others use Post-it notes or other forms of informal writing. Whatever form works for you, remember that when you put something in writing, it forces you to be mindful and

focused. Writing is an effective way to memorialize and reflect upon the good in your life.

♦ *Give a written gift* – Whether you are writing a formal letter, jotting a quick handwritten note, or sending an email, compliments and appreciations are powerful things. When we take the time to note and express appreciation, good things happen. The small act of leaving a note on a teacher's desk or placing it in their mailbox shows that you care about them and the work they are doing.

♦ *Schedule time for gratitude* – You schedule all the other important things in life, right? Why not plan a specific time each day to reflect on your blessings? We like to practice what we call "micro" moments of gratitude every day – short and simple moments where you collect your thoughts and focus on the blessings. You might also set aside a time each week for about ten minutes to close your office door and list and reflect upon all the ways you've been blessed.

♦ *Plan for staff gratitude* – This is a great practice to include in your staff meetings or professional trainings. Start your staff meeting with a gratitude activity and have a few individuals share. You might also have your staff "catch" others showing gratitude. Consider the use of a "Shout-Out" board where staff recognize their peers and are entered into a monthly drawing where both the giver and receiver are rewarded. The more you talk about it, model it, and use it, the more contagious it becomes. Over time, gratitude can also help to shift the culture of the school.

♦ *Shift the focus* – As educators, we tend to focus on areas of deficit when working with students. We are well trained to identify areas where students need to grow and then to create a plan for student success. Academically, this makes sense. We need to identify and close academic gaps for students. But when it comes to practicing resilience, a constant focus on deficits is problematic. In addition to addressing student gaps or challenges, ensure that time is spent discussing what students do well. Spend time discussing both strengths and weaknesses. Sentence starters are a great way to begin. Use starters such as "I am grateful for …" or "I appreciate this student for …".

◆ *Reflect and celebrate* – At the end of the day, it's important to reflect on your day and celebrate your successes. Be kind to yourself and remember that counting blessings and building resiliency is a shift in how we think. Speaking of reflection – keep an inventory of the good (the stories, the events, the blessings) and develop what Bryan (years ago) started referring to as an "I'm Great" file. It is exactly what it sounds like – a collection of notes, mementos, cards, etc. that remind you of the positive impact you are making. Include things like pictures students have drawn for you, notes of appreciation from staff, parents, and students, email communications that give evidence of your impact, etc. In essence, the "I'm Great" file is evidence of the positive impact you've had on your school or organization. And most importantly, occasionally pull out the file and review the evidence/artifacts as a nice boost to your resilience.

◆ *Get good sleep* – Before you go to sleep, reflect on the blessings and express gratitude for all that went well during the day. By the way, as an added bonus, there is evidence that gratitude can improve the quality of sleep (Wood et al., 2009). So, before you go to sleep, count blessings, not sheep.

3

Resilient School Leaders – Strive for a Work-Life Balance

In a Nutshell ✓

If we are not careful, being a school leader can engulf every aspect of our lives. While we should strive for excellence and give our very best to the organizations and the people we serve, we must also remember that a meaningful life involves career, family, faith, and community.

Digging Deeper 🔍

Regarding a work-life balance, organizational and time management expert Dr. Frank Buck (2018) asks an interesting question, "What do Bigfoot, the Loch Ness Monster, and work-life balance all have in common?" They are either elusive or don't exist at all! While we like to poke fun at the idea, it's actually quite a serious topic. Dr. Buck goes on to ask an important question – one that will help to shape our discussion here – "Would you know balance if you saw it?"

DOI: 10.4324/9781003301356-3

If you've never seen the circus act of plate spinning, go check out some video clips on the web. Once you view the art of balancing and spinning plates on tall, skinny poles, you'll likely say, "Yup. That's my life." Once we get some aspect of our lives under control, something else starts to wobble. With so many plates (responsibilities) spinning at the same time, we find ourselves running from emergency to emergency just trying to keep things from crashing to the ground. All this metaphorical running is exhausting.

Not that you necessarily need lots of convincing that work-life balance is important, but we thought you may find these things interesting:

- Even among school leaders who report high levels of job satisfaction, stress is still high (Darmody & Smyth, 2011).
- High levels of stress limit the effectiveness of school leaders (DeMatthews et al., 2021).
- The global coronavirus pandemic simultaneously highlighted and worsened the problem of stress among school leaders (Upadyaya et al., 2021).
- Even before the pandemic, school leaders reported that school-life balance was a significant stressor (De Jong et al., 2017).
- High stress (and how to manage it) among school leaders is not a new thing (Shoho & Barnett, 2010).

So, the question at hand is, *how do we keep a balance?* How do we give the best of ourselves to our schools, our families, and our community? Let's go back to the question posed by Dr. Buck, "Would you know work-life balance if you saw it?" Before we proceed to the Application Points, take a moment to describe your ideal work–life balance. Write it out. Be specific. Create a goal or two. The more you can be concrete about what work-life balance means to you, the more likely you'll strive to find it. By the way, if this reflective exercise is a bit of a challenge, ask those closest to you to help. Family, close friends, administrative assistants, and fellow leaders are good sources of feedback.

One last note – Why didn't we title this chapter, "Resilient school leaders **master** or **create** or **have** a work life balance?" The truth is, there are times when we simply cannot do it – getting ready for the first day of school, parent conferences, graduation, etc. Those are definitely times when you'll probably work far too many hours. But those times are limited; they are the exception not the rule.

Application Points

- *Remember your faith tradition* – Warren Bennis, 1990s leadership guru and author of books such as *On Becoming a Leader* (2009) and *Why Leaders Can't Lead* (1997), uses the term "reflective structures" – planned and purposeful opportunities to pause, reflect, and attend to spiritual needs. For many of us, this includes the structures, rhythms, and community offered by our faith.
- *Unplug* – The devices we've come to rely upon are great sources of … *distraction*. Yes, our phones and tablets and laptops can help us to be more productive, but they can also be terribly addicting and, if we are honest, they tether us to work regardless of where we are. If you struggle with unplugging or turning off your device, at the very least put the device on silent mode so you are not constantly distracted with alerts, pings, and noises. And don't send 4:00am emails to staff. That sends the wrong message.
- *Better yet, do a "digital detox"* – For an extended period of time, refrain from all screen time. In *Time* magazine's special edition *The Science of Happiness* (2020), Emma Seppala says, "One of the greatest ways to find joy is to spend a half day or a whole day on a technology fast. That means no screen time. None."
- *Be vulnerable* – Seek input from those who know you well – spouses, children, co-workers, mentors, and colleagues. Ask, "What signs do you see when the stress is getting to me?"

- *Make the time* – Resilient leaders are not too busy for the important things. They have and make time for what matters – that includes health (discussed in Chapter 1) but if also includes things like family time, reading for pleasure, professional learning, etc. In essence, it's a weak excuse to say "I'm too busy to …"
- *Tell people about your plans* – As you make plans and goals to live a balanced life, tell people. Telling others about your plans is powerful and helps to bring attention and focus to what matters most. If, for example, you make it a goal to leave the building by 5:00pm, tell your staff, family, and mentors. They may help to keep you accountable.
- *Remember the power of "no"* – We told you that this recommendation would keep showing up. Give careful consideration to those things that you add to your "plate". It's hard to live a balanced life if we keep saying yes to too many work-related responsibilities. You want to give your very best to your organization. That's a given. But you don't need to volunteer for every committee.
- *Get a mentor and be a mentor* – The authors of the book *Resilience: The Science of Mastering Life's Greatest Challenges* (2012) say it well, "Very few highly resilient individuals are strong in and by themselves."
- *Redefine "available"* – The idea that we need to "always be on" is not in the job description. Yes, you need to be available outside of school hours in case of emergencies. We've all gotten the dreaded call in the middle of the night when the building alarm is going off and you need to rush over to check it out. But those instances are rare. Being available in case of an emergency is not the same as being available at all hours of the day for things that are not emergencies.
- *Cultivate a non-education related interest* – Get a hobby, find an outlet for your creativity, or discover a hidden talent. On a regular basis, make the time to take your leadership hat off and just be a regular person.
- *Remember your real job* – Your to-do list is long and the day is short. As school leaders, most of our days are filled

with jumping from issue to issue, solving other peoples' problems. This is part of our jobs, of course. But, as we've pointed out, it can be exhausting. That, "You got a minute?" question rarely lasts a minute. So, by the end of the day you've done a good job helping others, but it can be easy to feel like you didn't get any of *your* work done. When those days happen, remember that your real job is leading and guiding people. Yes, you have tasks to complete and paperwork to finish and meetings to prepare for. But your most important job is giving attention to the people you lead.

◆ *But also remember that you are modeling for future leaders* – We have a teacher shortage and an administrator shortage. Quite simply, many younger people don't want to enter the leadership ranks. We need to make it appealing (beyond the paycheck). We are also modeling for our own children. As Janet reflected in the not-to-distant past, after she became an empty-nester, the number of hours available to work actually increased. She worked more hours and took on more long-term projects and then she had a big realization, "my 22 year-old daughter (who was just starting her career) was walking exactly in my footsteps. She was working way too many hours each week with little attention on herself and family. To make matters worse, I turned into 'that' mom sending her weekly (and sometimes daily) texts to remind her to eat every day and make that lingering doctor's appointment she was putting off. The reply I received from her was that she was just like me."

◆ *Decide* – As school leaders, rarely is there a day when we feel like we are all caught up. This is true of teachers as well, of course. But we need to make decisions about what gets done today and what can be done tomorrow. Quite simply, there needs to be an ending point of your workday. A specific time when you say, "I've done well today. It's time to stop working." This can be a challenge for many reasons. One – there is always more to do. Two – many of us have offices at home. So we work at school and we work at home. Starting today, be intentional about your work schedule. It's okay to turn off school in order to focus on yourself. Whether that means being present with family, exercising, or just sitting in quiet, you need to be intentional in making time for yourself ... no guilt!

◆ *Empower and delegate* – You hire the best people you can find. Hire them, train them, and then let them do their jobs. People want to be empowered and they want to be trusted to do good work. Let them do it. By the way, if you are a micromanager, you'll struggle with this recommendation. But, if you are a micromanager, challenge yourself to think differently. Micromanaging things that don't need to be micromanaged is very stressful. It simply adds unnecessary tasks to your workload.

◆ *Tame email* – An *Education Week* article titled, "I Want a Job and a Life: How Principals Find Balance in All-Consuming Work" (Superville, 2018), offers some pointed and necessary advice, "Be disciplined about email, only reading and responding at specific times. Don't respond immediately, or people will expect instant replies. Set an outgoing message that says you're in classrooms and directs people to other staff who can help. And, the fewer emails you send, the fewer you will receive."

4

Resilient School Leaders – Focus on Purpose

In a Nutshell ✅

A clear purpose – one that can be defined, discussed, and articulated – provides clarity during times of stress and can help to focus our efforts, energy, and tasks on those things that are most likely to produce the best results.

Digging Deeper 🔍

To start, we need to define some intertwined and often-confused terms: *vision*, *mission*, and *purpose*.

- ◆ An organization's *vision* is a statement about the future. It's a declaration about what the future should look like if the organization is effectively working towards its mission. The vision answers the question, "What does our ideal future look like?"

DOI: 10.4324/9781003301356-4

◆ An organization's *mission* focuses on how the vision is going to become a reality. It focuses on action and answers the question, "How will we do this?"

◆ A *purpose* is the reason for the work. It's focused on answering the question, "Why do this work?" Purpose provides meaning. Having a clear meaning helps to build a bridge between the present (and its challenges) and a future (focused on hope and vision).

Mission and vision are typically organizational in nature. The school, district, or organization you work for has probably already created a mission and a vision. Mission and vision statements should extend throughout the organization and are often posted in hallways, offices, and on websites. They should be understood and known to all who work in the organization, particularly those in leadership. Mission and vision statements are also typically stable, lasting years, if not decades with very little change.

Purpose, on the other hand, is personal. This is not to say that organizations don't have a purpose. They do. For example, Toms Shoes has a clear purpose – to build a more equitable world by donating one third of corporate profits to grassroots causes. But for our discussion here, the key difference is that a purpose can, and typically is, personal. For example, people can have very different purposes for being in leadership yet still believe in and support an organization's vision and mission.

It is important to note that just having a clear purpose is not enough. We've often heard the sentiment that "just focus on your purpose" and everything will work out. Just focusing on purpose may not be enough. In fact, as we'll discuss more in Chapter 12, even those who have a clear purpose, are still vulnerable to burnout.

And here is a recipe for happiness – when we can work in an organization where we believe in the vision and mission and we can act out our personal purpose for being a leader or educator. If you've been blessed to work in such an environment, you know how empowering it is to go to work. If you've worked in an organization where your personal purpose does not align well to the organization's mission and vision, you know how stressful it can be.

Meaning and purpose are inter-related. In *The Resilience Workbook* (2017), Glenn Schiraldi discusses how the two relate to each other. Purpose, he says, focuses on what you are determined to do. It consists of your goals and what you intend to accomplish. Meaning, on other the other hand, relates to how a person's actions are worthwhile and significant to the individual. As an exercise, Schiraldi suggests that you write a job description for your current position. Write it in a way that would make people want to apply for it. Highlight the best aspects of the job and the true joys that come along with it. If this exercise is a struggle, by the way, you may be in a job that does not align well to your personal purpose.

The necessity of a leader having a clear purpose is the central theme of Simon Sinek's 2011 bestselling book *Start with Why: How Great Leaders Inspire Everyone to Take Action*. Using concentric circles, Sinek outlines what he refers to as the basics of human (and organizational) behavior by describing the differences between *WHAT* we do, *HOW* we do it, and *WHY* we do it. The *WHAT* is the work (being a school principal, for example). The *HOW* is focused on the methods used to tackle the work. Those are the first two circles. The *WHY* is the purpose or reason for doing the work; this is the last and innermost circle. Most organizations, he points out, start from the outside and work inwards. But great leaders and successful organizations work from the inside out. We start with a clear why – a clear purpose – and align the What and How to that clear purpose. Among the points he makes is:

- ◆ When we have a clear purpose (he calls it the WHY – all caps), it's easier to enjoy the work.
- ◆ Having a clear purpose provides clarity, particularly during times of high stress and conflict. A clear purpose is empowering.
- ◆ A clear purpose builds trust with those you are attempting to lead.
- ◆ Why is a process of discovery.

This last point – *Why is a process of discovery* – requires some explanation. Great leaders don't find their purpose, they develop it. That's the contention of John Coleman (2018), who says that purpose is something that we build, craft, and create. It's not something that is magically or mystically bestowed upon us.

So, why do effective leaders focus on purpose? Vision and mission statements can change over time or change when you switch to work in a different organization. Your purpose probably stays consistent. Your purpose, your why (and the meaning that comes from doing purposeful work) is empowering, exciting, and motivating. Leadership strategies, instructional methods, curricula, technology, and organizational structures will change. That's why we focus on purpose. We live for purpose; we don't live for those things that often change.

Before you jump to the Application Points, here is the most essential strategy of the chapter. If you've not done so recently, take a few minutes and distill your purpose down to a concrete statement of one to two sentences. Once you've done so, print it out and share it. Discuss it and get feedback from those you trust. If this is a struggle, consider tackling the task by answering the following questions: (Hedges, 2018)

- ◆ What are you good at doing?
- ◆ What do you enjoy doing?
- ◆ What feels most useful?
- ◆ What creates a sense of forward momentum?

In his quirky but insightful book simply titled *The Brain Book* (2016), author Phil Dobson states it directly, "You are more resilient when you feel you have a purpose, and more resourceful when you are making progress towards objectives that you find meaningful. If you feel stressed or you're having a rough time, remind yourself of the reasons you're doing what you're doing." In addition, having a clear purpose also helps with health and longevity. A 2014 study found that those who had a sense of purpose for their lives had a 15% lower risk of an early death (Hill & Turiano, 2014).

You may also benefit from examples written by others. Below we've included ours and we've provided some samples collected from various sources:

◆ Bryan's purpose statement is: *To honor God and my family and strive to better the lives of students and teachers.*

◆ Janet's purpose statement is: *To inspire learning through kindness, compassion, perseverance, and engagement.*

◆ From the website happierhuman.com:

• I am dedicated to working on behalf of children, to bring them the resources they need for a healthy and prosperous present and future life.

• To lead by example, personifying my values of kindness, forgiveness, compassion, empathy, and hard work.

• To make the world a better place for individuals with special needs, by participating in initiatives that focus on inclusivity and strengths recognition.

◆ From Indeed.com:

• To be a teacher and inspire my students to be the best version of themselves.

• To give students the resources and attention they need to grow into confident, effective adults.

• To educate young minds and create compassionate, empathetic and hard-working members of society.

One more note – it's OK if the process of drafting and revising a personal purpose statement is a bit messy. That's to be expected if you've not created one before. Elena Aguilar (2018) says that resilient educators stay grounded in purpose. Our purpose drives our energy. When you can, at the end of a long day, say, "I'm exhausted but I'm doing what I'm born to do" – that is your purpose.

Application Points

◆ *Regularly reflect on your purpose* – How might you answer the following questions?

- "Do you know your purpose for being a leader?"
- "Can you clearly state your purpose in one to two sentences?"
- "How is having a clear purpose connected to your ability to manage stress?"
- "In what ways did I fulfill my purpose today?"

◆ *Keep it simple* – As you strive to create and refine your purpose, keep it simple. A sentence, maybe two, is adequate. Any more than that and it's likely to be forgotten or too elaborate to be useful. In addition, purpose statements tend to be stable over time; you'll likely make subtle changes in wording or phrases over time, but the essential foundation of a purpose will likely not change much from year to year.

◆ *Help your staff create their purpose* – Lead them through the process of drafting a purpose statement and help them to understand how a focus on purpose can help to manage stress.

◆ *Make fewer things relevant* – This is easier said than done, of course. But remember that stress is related to relevance in this sense – if something is relevant in my life and I can control it, my stress is low. If something is relevant and I cannot control it, stress is high. So, the fewer things that I deem relevant, the fewer things that can cause me stress. Your perception of control is possibly the most powerful stress reliever you have at your disposal.

◆ *Keep an "I'm Great" file* – As suggested in the previous chapter, create an "I'm Great" file. Start a collection of artifacts (notes, pictures, written reflections, evaluations, kudos, and appreciations such as thank you notes) that remind you of why you are a leader and the difference that you've made in peoples' lives. Why do we do this? There are simply some days when you need to be reminded of the positive impact you've had on people. The "I'm Great" file is the place to find those reminders.

◆ *Remind yourself of your purpose when things get challenging* – Having a clear, articulable purpose helps with decision making, particularly during times of transition, difficulty, change, or confusion.

♦ *Don't fall into the trap that our purpose is the same as our job description* – It's not. We are not suggesting that a job description is a bad thing. Of course we need clear job descriptions. But meeting the criteria of a job description does not necessarily mean that we are meeting our purpose. Your job or your job title is not your purpose.

♦ *Find small changes* – Angela Duckworth, in her 2016 book *Grit: The Power of Passion and Perseverance,* addresses the role of purpose in tackling life's obstacles. She recommends the following reflective exercise to help clarify your purpose: Consider the small but meaningful changes you can make to your current work that will enhance your purpose.

♦ *Get into classrooms* – That's where all our efforts pay off. Getting into classrooms is also a way to get ahead of the stress – it's preventative in nature. Schedule this on your calendar and make time in classrooms with students and teachers a priority. As Bryan's long-time superintendent and mentor often said, "You were not hired to lead from behind a desk."

♦ *Learn with purpose in mind* – Knowledge without purpose is pointless. Learning new things is great. In fact, if we are not learning and growing, we quickly become stagnant and irrelevant. But unless we have a solid grasp on our purpose, any new learning is unlikely to make much of a difference.

5

Resilient School Leaders – Are Self-Aware

In a Nutshell ☑

Effective leaders are aware of their skills, habits, tendencies, and pet peeves. Highly self-aware leaders are conscious of how those things impact the people around them and consistently work to become more self-aware.

Digging Deeper 🔍

First of all, we want to acknowledge that leadership is not easy. Good leaders make it look easy, but it's a lot of work. It's a daily balance (a dance really) of confidence, character, and control. And we need to maintain that delicate balance while making quick decisions that can potentially impact lots of people. This leadership thing is not for the faint of heart and it can, at times, be overwhelming. Within that hustle and bustle of each school day, we may lack awareness of how we feel, act, and interact with others. An increased self-awareness can help us to manage stress because it helps us to realize (become aware) of how we

DOI: 10.4324/9781003301356-5

impact others. That awareness is the first step towards action (taking control) in order to practice resilience and manage stress.

The term self-awareness refers to an understanding of the emotional state we are in, how we think, and how we behave. When we are self-aware, we are able to regulate ourselves and be comfortable with who we are. Think about the saying that hindsight is 20/20. It's great to reflect and understand a situation that has already happened but thinking about the current situation you are in and being aware of your present behavior is what builds resiliency.

Part of being self-aware is knowing your own worth. This means that we don't constantly look to others for validation. Validation is fine. We all appreciate moments of recognition from others. But our worth is not or cannot be caught up in what others think or feel because what other people think is subject to change. A lot. In addition, what other people think is not always true, valid, or logical.

Self-awareness and knowing your worth centers on the ability to comprehend and consider not only your strengths but your tendencies, habits, and challenges/weaknesses. There can actually be a sense of pride in knowing who you are, what you've made of yourself, and of your accomplishments. Keep in mind that pride does not have to equate to arrogance. It merely means identifying and acknowledging your areas of strength and talent as well as areas that you need to improve.

When I am aware of my own worth and value (and recognize that my value is rooted in something deeper than my current circumstances), it is easier to accept responsibility for my mistakes. And, when I am aware (and take time to acknowledge) my own strengths and weaknesses, I can appreciate the strengths of others and provide grace for their weaknesses. In essence, I know who I am and I'm not intimidated by the talents of others. I know who I am and I know what I'm good at and what I'm not. Why does this matter? Quite simply, most of us are unaware of our thinking patterns, including negative ones (Margolis & Stoltz, 2018). Becoming self-aware requires us to acknowledge and act upon both our strengths and our weaknesses.

Another element of self-awareness is understanding how other people see you. Individuals that recognize how others view them are more likely to show empathy and value others' perspectives (Eurich, 2018). This, by the way, is a significant step in building positive relationships with staff, students, and parents. Take the time to talk to the people around you. Get their perspective on things like how you behave or act in certain situations. Or what communication habits or tendencies you have. Most of us like to think we are fairly self-aware. And, honestly, most of us probably are. But being an effective leader requires humility. We all have our tendencies, flaws, and habits that can negatively impact our effectiveness. Ask others for input in order to become more self-aware. Here is a good place to start, ask your secretary or office staff, "How do I typically respond when someone gives me bad news?" We can't become more resilient unless we are aware of our typical reactions. Eurich (2018) also found that leaders that have self-awareness tend to have greater job satisfaction, more personal control, stronger relationships, and more happiness. In the long run, understanding yourself will help you grow into a more resilient leader.

We realize that being conscious of yourself takes work and requires external feedback and opens you up for criticism. However, the outcomes of being self-aware far outweigh the unconscious behaviors you experience when you are not aware. It's about managing your emotional state and knowing what you are capable of. And, when you think about it, every day you are asking your students, staff, and families to be more self-aware of how their behavior impacts others. We need to do the same.

Along these same lines, resilient school leaders know how to handle disappointment. In some ways, we need to become masters of rejection. We get told "no" a lot. In fact, Richard Davidson, neuroscientist and author of the book *The Emotional Life of Your Brain* (2012) suggests that a great way to gauge your personal resilience is by reflecting on how you respond when things don't go your way. He goes on to suggest that how we respond to the little things strongly predicts how we'll respond to the big things.

Finally, remember that part of being self-aware is taking time to do what James Flaherty, author of *Coaching: Evoking Excellence in Others* (2005) calls self-observation. He contends that all change begins with an examination of self. This examination involves daily and/or weekly reflections on accomplishments, emotional responses, successes, and breakdowns. He suggests that leaders reflect on questions such as:

- How did I take care of myself today?
- What part of my life did I ignore or avoid this week?
- At what did I become more competent?
- What energized me at work today?
- What discouraged me at work today?
- What made me feel uncomfortable?
- What did I insist upon?

Application points

- *Create "I believe" statements* – Stanford professor Robert Sutton (2007) found that highly successful organizations have a "no jerks" culture where leaders' beliefs align with how others see them. In other words, don't say one thing and do another. To prevent sending the wrong message, create "I believe" statements to identify what it is that you truly believe about subjects such as teaching, learning, conflict, growth, acceptance, humility, and forgiveness. Then, make sure that your management practices follow what you believe and practice at your school.
- *Jot it down* – It's important to self-reflect on what is important to you. Knowing your wants, needs, goals, and aspirations (as well as areas needed for growth) will help you to evaluate your own abilities and consider where action is most necessary.
- *Reflect* – We learn from reflecting on an experience, and not just from the experience itself. Aguilar (2018) explained it well when reflecting upon the challenges of the global pandemic. She explains, "We know from research that we build resilience when we go through rough times and emerge stronger than before – yet sometimes we don't recognize that growth unless we stop, look back, feel the

emotions that arise, and process them." Take the time. Look back and reflect. Then make a plan for moving forward.

♦ *Reframe* – The "father" of American Psychology William James once said, "The greatest weapon against stress is our ability to choose one thought over another." That's the essence of reframing. It's when we elect to think about, process, or talk about a situation we are facing from a different, more positive perspective. When you find yourself in a negative state or thinking pattern, take efforts to think about them differently. Become aware and then take action.

♦ *Seek candid feedback* – As a school leader, everyone has an opinion about how you are doing your job. We suggest that you seek feedback from those that you have a good relationship with and that you know will be honest with you. Feedback is not about judgement, it's about action. It's about where you can take action in order to improve an outcome.

♦ *Seek help* – Know when to get help. All leaders experience stress but knowing ourselves well enough to say "this is just too much" is really important. We all have times when we need to seek professional help in order to gain perspective. Seeking help is a sign of strength, not a sign of weakness.

♦ *Record yourself* – One of the best ways to critic your inter-action with others is to record it. Of course, you will need to get permission from all participants, but using this method will give you a chance to actually see or hear yourself from a different perspective. After all, have you ever heard yourself on a recording (like a voice mail) and asked, "Do I really sound like that?" How we "sound" to ourselves may be very different than how we sound to others. So, get some data via a recording of some type and then reflect in private. Find something you can improve and set a specific goal for changing one thing at a time.

♦ *Find balance* – Depending on the situation, you may be too assertive or not assertive enough, or you may be overly confident when you should be a bit more humble. As you reflect and hear from others, seek that "just right" balance where the "how" you do things is just as important as "why" you do them.

◆ *Take a self-awareness quiz* – Taking a quiz will help you to become more in tune with our feelings and behaviors. Just being aware of what you believe will help you regulate your emotions, especially when you get into a difficult situation. Along those same lines, you may be unaware of your own stress levels and how that stress is impacting you and the people around you. Consider taking something like the PSS – *Perceived Stress Scale* – developed by Carnegie Mellon and the University of Oregon. Or check out any of the excellent resources developed by the American Institute of Stress at www.stress.org.

◆ *Ask, "What do I believe about people"?* – An interesting and enlightening exercise comes from Leonard Pellicer's book *Caring Enough to Lead* (2008). He suggests that leaders take time to ponder the question, "What do I believe about people?" As a reflection on human nature, are they basically good, caring, and altruistic? Or are most people lazy and only out for themselves. Of course, at any given moment, we all fall somewhere on a good to not-so-good spectrum. But what do we believe about people in general? Why is this important? Pellicer points out that most of us (especially those in leadership) will tend to find what we are looking for. If you believe that people are basically good, helpful, and kind, you'll tend to see examples of that in your daily life. The opposite is also true.

6

Resilient School Leaders – Are Mindful

In a Nutshell ☑

Becoming more mindful is a powerful and effective way to manage stress and build resilience. Mindfulness forces us to attend to the present moment in order to consciously and intentionally do our best to lead and guide others. In essence, mindfulness helps us to bring our "A Game" to each unique situation.

Digging Deeper 🔍

It's likely that when you first started hearing about resilience, stress management, or self-care that you also heard about the concept of mindfulness. The concepts seem so intertwined that they've practically become synonymous. Among some who research and write about self-care or resiliency-building, they talk about mindfulness as if it were the Holy Grail of stress management. Mindfulness, it turns out *is* a significant and powerful way to manage stress and build resilience, but it may not be what you think it is.

DOI: 10.4324/9781003301356-6

To start, let's dispel a common myth: *mindfulness is not the same as meditation*. This myth, by the way, is one of the reasons that some people shy away from the concept of mindfulness. They assume that in order to be mindful you need to adopt the difficult practice of meditation. Or that you need to begin yoga or adopt certain mystical eastern religious practices. That's not the case. Mindfulness can actually be quite simple. By the way, we are not against meditation or yoga; they work well for some people. But there are lots of ways to bring mindfulness into your daily life.

So, then, what does it mean to be mindful? What does mindfulness look like for a busy school leader? And how might mindfulness help us manage our daily stressors and challenges?

A solid definition would be good place to start. Mindfulness is the art of experiencing something fully, in the moment. It's about being present and not overly focusing on either the past (and its mistakes) or the future (and its worries). It works because it takes us to the here and now (where we have control) instead of to the past or future (where we don't). At its core, mindfulness is being aware and bringing to conscious thought what you are experiencing. It's willful, intentional thought. It's the habit of being aware of one's current state of mind (your thoughts, emotions, reactions, and tendencies) and the state of your body (posture, breathing, tension, etc.).

Ellen Petry Leanse, in her book *The Happiness Hack* (2017), puts it this way, "We can think of mindfulness as the act of interrupting the brain's tendency towards routine, reactive, and fast processing. Instead, we shift, intentionally, to aware, directed thinking." That is, we slow down and become mindful/aware of what is happening in the current moment.

The concept of mindfulness has received a lot of attention in the last few years. It's difficult, in fact, to discuss resilience or stress management without someone mentioning it. While it's gotten a lot of press as of late, it's not a new concept. In fact, back in 2007, renowned UCLA researcher Dr. Daniel Siegel, published *The Mindful Brain*. Although he most commonly uses the term *mindful awareness* or *attunement* (and his more recent work centers on the concept of *presence*), the idea is that we benefit greatly from mindfulness. Furthermore, Dr. Siegel points out that mindfulness can be cultivated and improved with intentionality.

If you haven't yet considered why being mindful is essential for a school leader, let's connect some dots. Being fully present and aware of the moment is necessary for things like: completing staff evaluations, working with students who present challenging behaviors, talking with an upset parent about a controversial topic, learning a new curriculum, or developing a new skill. All of those examples require that our brains fully attend to the present moment in order to learn, lead, help, or solve problems. Being mindful means that we don't default to habits, past experiences, or prior assumptions. Mindfulness requires that we strive to give each experience, challenge, or situation our full attention.

You might be thinking, "I'm pretty good at being aware of my thinking patterns and emotional responses. I think I'm pretty mindful." Well, according to a 2010 Harvard study people, on average, spend about 47% of their time thinking about something other than what they are actually doing. Our brains are on autopilot much of the time. Being intentionally mindful takes effort. But that effort is necessary in order to simultaneously lead others and to manage our own stress.

Mindfulness forces us to slow down. To take note – to appreciate, to reflect. If we are always in a hurry – going from one task to the next (even when we are being efficient), it's tough to be mindful. And here is the real challenge of being a mindful school leader – you are likely *always* in a hurry! Your to-do list is always longer than your *to-done* list. If it seems like you can never get ahead, let's talk about that.

Being in a hurry steals our attention away from the present moment in order to focus on the future or in order to get something accomplished; to get something checked off that ever-growing to-do list. While a focus on the future (what needs to be done) is not necessarily a bad thing, people need us to be present – in the moment – and not preoccupied with what's next. You've had those social interactions with distracted people, right? Maybe it was a supervisor or a parent or a student. You needed them to be present and to fully engage with you but their attention was elsewhere. It's frustrating. Now consider this – as school leaders, that often describes us. We are physically present but mentally elsewhere.

In the 2019 book *The Ruthless Elimination of Hurry*, pastor John Mark Comer, challenges us to slow down and consider the toll that the "always in a hurry, always needing to do more" mentality takes on us. See if you can find yourself in a description of his own life:

> My life is so fast. And I like fast. I'm type A. Driven. A get-crap-done kind of guy. But we're well past that now. I work six days a week, early to late, and it's still not enough time to get it all done. Worse, I feel hurried. Like I'm tearing through each day, so busy with life that I'm missing out on the moment. And what is life but a series of moments?

Mindfulness, by definition and in application, forces us to slow down, to consider the present moment, and to think critically about each unique situation in front of us. Pastor Comer goes on to challenge us to slow down – to truly slow down – in order to reset and focus on the things that matter the most. He asks, "Is busyness your default setting?" If it is, the Application Points we outline below are a great starting point.

You might be interested to know that there is a solid foundation of research that suggests mindfulness has a positive impact on mental health and stress management (otherwise, we would not have included the concept in this book). Among the most powerful effects of mindfulness include: decreased episodes of depression, improvement in self-control, and improved immunity (Keng et al., 2011). The United States military even has a resiliency-building program for its troops. That training program includes mindfulness as a significant component. If you want to do your own deeper dive, we'll point you to the work of the Greater Good Science Center based out of the University of California at Berkeley. They offer cutting-edge research and insights into what mindfulness, gratitude, and resilience.

Side note – we elected to title this chapter "Resilient School Leaders **Are** Mindful" instead "Resilient School Leaders Practice Mindfulness." Mindfulness is something that we are intentional about throughout the day in order to effectively lead. It's what we intend to *be* rather than what we intend to *do*. This nuance might seem inconsequential but it's important. When something is a "practice" it implies a specific place or a routine. Meditation, as we discussed in the opening of the chapter, is a practice. Again, we are not anti-meditation. Many people find it to a wonderful way to manage stress. But if we add another practice, another thing you need to do, well ... you know how to end that sentence. It's stressful to add another thing to your already too-busy life. While there are specific "practices" (we call them Application Points), the key idea is that when we lead others, the goal is to do so in a mindful, in-the-moment, and fully-present way.

Application Points

- ◆ *Start with reflection* – Begin each day with a moment of reflection and introspection. Ask, "How am I feeling today?" or "What is my underlying mood?" This matters because our moods impact how we treat others. Our moods influence our patience levels, what we notice in our environment, and how we talk to ourselves about challenges.

- ◆ *Embrace and plan for silence and stillness* – Moments of silence and solitude can offer opportunities to reflect and reset. As school leaders we are busy; there's lots to do and lots to get done. Create time in your daily schedule to be mindful of what you are doing and how you are doing it. We were not hired merely to do lots of things. We were hired to do the right kinds of things that get the right kinds of results. When we take moments to be mindful of what we are doing – to stop being busy for just a few minutes – we can reflect on our impact and take a moment to consider how we are dealing with our stressors. Don't be afraid of silence; it can offer you the opportunity to reflect.

◆ *Challenge the assumption that "busy" equals "productive"* – If you've not thought about this subtle difference before, it's an interesting discussion. You were hired to get results. We can all agree on that. And you're an achiever – you've gotten stuff done in the past. That's why you were hired and trusted to lead a school or an organization. So, our underlying, often un-discussed, assumption is that we've got to go, go, go all day long. It's exhausting, really. It's why so many of us burnout, become cynical, or simply ineffective. Too many of us have bought into the lie that we must constantly be doing and going and be busy in order to do our jobs. Obviously, we can't lead very effectively if we are lazy, but we may need to reconsider the idea that just because we are busy it means that we are doing something good. We are reminded of a famous quote from Corrie ten Boom, "If the devil cannot make us bad, he will make us busy."

◆ *Slow down when you eat* – Take the time to actually taste your food. Appreciate flavors, textures, the experience. For many busy school leaders, eating a meal is a luxury we don't have time for. But being aware – being mindful – of the food you consume (including the quality and quantity of the food) is an easy way to be mindful. Instead of mindlessly scarfing down an energy bar and a Diet Coke at lunch, attend to and think about what you eat. This habit, by the way, is a good way to consider a refinement in your diet in order to "put your mask on first" as we discussed in Chapter 1.

◆ *Slow down when you ...* – You've no doubt seen a theme here – mindfulness requires that we slow down and intentionally tune in to the situations in front of us. This is important because, although you've likely dealt with similar situations in the past, each person and context is unique. Our goal is to give our attention (in essence – our best) when we *talk* with others, *read* important work, *think* about goals and actions, and when we *write* or communicate essential ideas. We might even want to slow down when we *walk*.

◆ *Go for a walk* – Speaking of walking, get outside and notice, appreciate, and take in the beauty and uniqueness of your surroundings. Leave the cell phone in your office, tell your office staff that you'll be outside for a few minutes and walk your campus.

◆ *Breathe* – A common suggestion to manage stress is to initiate some breathing exercises during stressful times. But it turns out that the kind of breathing matters. The way we breathe can either initiate a stress reaction or it can help to calm us down. You read that correctly, the wrong kind of breathing can actually cause us to be *more* stressed. Author James Nestor, in the 2020 book, *Breath*, provides several practical suggestions. Most notably, breathing deeply in through the nose and holding the breath for a few seconds before exhaling is a good start. To learn more about the power of breathing, we'll point you to www.breatheforchange.com/.

◆ *Read* – In order to get the most out of a book like this (or any book for that matter), you've got to force yourself to be mindful. And it's a constant challenge, isn't it? Especially if you are reading this book as part of a book study with a deadline. You'll get the most out of reading (particularly technical or work-related topics) when you force yourself to be present and fully dig in. That means that you need to resist the temptation to multitask (which the brain can't really do anyway) by turning off the devices and putting yourself in an environment or context that is conducive to reading. And if you think about it, "getting lost in a good book" is one of the reasons so many of us love novels.

◆ *Speaking of getting lost, try reading poetry* – That's an odd suggestion for busy school leaders, isn't it? And we'll admit, poetry isn't our go-to medium of the written word. But think about what poetry forces you do. In order to fully comprehend and appreciate poetry, you must consider words, imagery, patterns, and nuance. For most of us, this requires that we slow down to fully understand the message of the poem.

◆ *Become a beginner at something* – Learn a new language, blow the dust off that violin you haven't touched since 8th grade, learn a computer coding language, or take a welding class at a local community college. In essence, do what you are asking your students to do every day – learn a new skill, habit, or knowledge base. When we are beginners, we must by necessity slow down and become mindful about what we are learning.

◆ *Play board games* – Some of our suggestions here take additional time and effort. We get that. But to be mindful requires that we invest time and effort. But that time and effort does not always have to be challenging (like learning a new language) or deeply introspective (like reading poetry). Play games – especially new ones that you've never played before. Learning the rules, directions, and strategies of a new game forces you to be mindful. And when you can have fun being mindful, that's even better!

◆ *Do a digital detox* – Our phones and devices can certainly help us to be more efficient, but they might not be helping us be more mindful. Consider time in your daily or weekly schedule to set aside the devices in order to find time to begin some of the previous Application Points. If you are not sure you can set aside the device, ask yourself, "Is this device *saving* me time or is it *taking* my time?" While we are speaking about the smartphones, have you considered this – it doesn't actually work for you. You pay for it. But it works for Apple, or Samsung, or Google. It is constantly collecting data and reporting to its owner. All that data it collects is used to send you advertisements and offers and distractions. Being inundated with all that data makes focus even more difficult. Basically, it's your attention that's for sale.

◆ *Recognize* – We can't always be mindful, of course. It's impossible to be mindful 100% of our waking hours. Our goal is to be mindful when it matters most. During times of stress, conflict, or challenge, it is easy to default to old habits or prior ways to dealing with issues. That might work much of the time. But we do best to recognize the moments that need us to be fully present.

♦ *Can I take my time?* – "Very little can be done with hurry that can't be done better without it." That's the reminder of John Comer in *The Ruthless Elimination of Hurry* (2019). Can we be a bit vulnerable for a moment? The submission of this manuscript was several months late. Why? We needed to slow down and take stock of what really mattered – what really needed to be included in this book and what didn't. The "we" by the way, in the previous sentence is in reference to Bryan. I found myself feeling rushed even though it was a self-imposed manuscript deadline. And our editor Lauren is first-class ... patient, understanding, helpful. But I found myself focused more on getting it done than doing it well. When I slowed down and fully re-engaged in the writing of this book, it became more enjoyable, and (if I do say so myself) it turned out pretty good.

7

Resilient School Leaders – Prioritize Relationships

In a Nutshell ✅

Strong, trusting, and honest relationships offer us support, encouragement, feedback, and the occasional kick in the pants we need in order to be personally healthy and resilient and to effectively lead others. Success in any aspect of life is rarely achieved all by ourselves.

Digging Deeper 🔍

You probably don't need to be convinced that relationships matter. After all, we are in a profession that focuses on the development of people. We are in the people business. To be successful in the "people" business, we need to establish, maintain, strengthen, and sometimes repair relationships. But, you likely know all that already. Our focus here is a reminder and elaboration upon *why* and *how* positive relationships help us to manage the stressors we experience on the job.

DOI: 10.4324/9781003301356-7

In case you do want to know a bit more about the *what* of relationships – what positive relationships produce in our lives – here is a short list of some of the more interesting findings from research:

- ◆ Having a positive network of family, friends, and colleagues supports the immune system (Sapolsky, 2004).
- ◆ Workplace environments that have positive relationships produce increased job satisfaction (Mansfield et al., 2014).
- ◆ Positive relationships result in longer life (Holt-Lunstad et al., 2010).
- ◆ Merely thinking about the positive relationships in your life can help to manage stressful times (Bourassa et al., 2019).
- ◆ In one of the most seminal, long-term studies ever conducted on the connection between health outcomes and relationships (known as the Grant and Glueck studies from Harvard University), researchers found that long, happy, and healthy lives required positive relationships at each stage of life.

Throughout the book we've referred to various definitions of stress and resilience and we've offered different analogies and ways of thinking about these intertwined concepts. Let's add a bit more depth to the conversation – we can think of resilience as related to specific conditions or factors in a person's life.

In one of the first in-depth and long-term studies of resilience, researchers Emmy Werner and Ruth Smith (1992) followed the lives of more than 500 men and women born on the Hawaiian island of Kauai in 1955. Sometimes referred to as The Kauai Study, Werner and Smith followed the lives of these individuals for decades (some of them from birth through age 40+) looking at their quality of life as measured by things such as health outcomes, school difficulties, relationships successes such as marriage and divorce rates, and they even looked at data related to substances abuses.

What they found, among other things, was that many children (about one third in this study) who were born into challenging and difficult circumstances actually ended up thriving in life. That is, they overcame the odds of being born into stressful environments that included high levels of poverty. That's actually what Werner and Smith ended up titling their 1992 book – *Overcoming the Odds*. They found that when children (and adults, too) had protective factors in their lives, they on average, did quite well in life. They overcame the stressors (the risk factors) because they had host of protective factors that provided a defensive shield allowing them to thrive in life. And, as you've likely already guessed, one of the primary protective factors in someone's life is the quality and depth of the relationships they have.

Max Depree, in the book *Leadership is an Art* (2004) reminds us that, "the only way we stand a chance of reaching our potential is first to gain competence in our relationships." He goes on to say that relationships matter more than structure. Sure, structures and systems matter. But people matter more. If we are honest with ourselves, some of us are really, really good at creating systems and plans and structures for how our schools should operate. In the midst of creating those things, we must remember to attend to people. After all, it's the people who implement our systems.

As a school leader, you no doubt tell your teachers to establish strong relationships with students and families. You advise them to do things like, stand at the door and greet students, express an interest in student's lives outside of the classroom, share stories, and make positive phone calls home. Those things matter tremendously. Student-teacher bonds are essential. And so are the bonds that teachers and students have with their leaders.

By way of reflection and application (before we get to the Application Points below), consider the state or status of the various relationships in your life with this framework: *establish, maintain, strengthen,* and *repair.* There are some people or groups that you need to *establish* a connection with. Other relationships need *maintenance.* Still others need to be *strengthened* and we sometimes need to *repair* relationships when some harm has been done. Take a moment to consider which relationships fall into those different categories and then take the necessary action to improve those relationships. Because, as you'll remember, taking action is a way to manage stress.

One final note – a personal story (from Bryan). When I first became a school principal, I was pretty good at establishing connections and relationships with people. I was (and I still am, I think) personable, relatable, and genuinely interested in people. Like most of you, those things came pretty naturally. What I was ill-prepared for was the sheer amount of time it took to establish connections and bonds *with so many people*. I didn't have a huge staff, mind you; about 30 teachers and about half that number in other staff members. But then there were students, parents, colleagues from other schools, and the larger community. It was, at times, overwhelming to think about where I'd find the time to connect with so many people. And, as we all know, some of the people that I needed to connect with were just not all that interesting or enjoyable to be around. There were other people that I really enjoyed spending time with but they just wanted too much of it; there were days when I got nothing done but talk to people. I share the story just to acknowledge that it's hard to connect and bond with lots of people. But it's necessary in order to be an effective leader.

Application Points

- ◆ *Curate your critics* – We're not sure where we first heard that advice, but there is a deep truth in the admonition to be cautious about who you take advice and criticism from. Find people who will tell you the truth and be honest with you but be careful about who you let into that select group. They'll have an impact on you – either good or bad. There is truth to the statement that *we become like who we hang out with*.
- ◆ *Recognize CAVE people* – Every staff and organization has them – *colleagues against virtually everything*. You know who they are. You're probably stifling a laugh right now just thinking about them. While you likely can't avoid them all the time, you can limit your exposure to them and be aware of how they might be influencing your thinking patterns or emotional responses.

◆ *Finish this sentence* – "Because I have developed strong relationships with staff, students, and families, I can …". This reflective activity allows us to consider options and opportunities that we may not have yet fully realized.

◆ *Get a coach or mentor* – This suggestion appears other times in this book because it's an important strategy. We all need people who we can confide in; people who will help guide us through difficult times. Here's another way to think about it – even the best athletes in the world still have coaches. Consider who you think is the GOAT (greatest of all time) in your favorite sport. That GOAT still has a coach (or a team of coaches) even though they are better and more accomplished than the people who are coaching them. Everyone, regardless of how good they are, benefits from a different perspective. We all benefit from a coach or a mentor even when we are proficient and "good" at our jobs.

◆ *Find a non-education related peer group* – Establish relationships with people outside the profession. For some of us it's connecting with a group that has a hobby we enjoy. Others might want to connect with civic organizations or faith-based institutions. Whether it be a fun hobby, a physical activity, a book club, or a community-based group, spend time with people outside of the profession.

◆ *Be proactive* – When you find yourself struggling with certain stressors (dealing with difficult people, for example … a topic we discuss in Chapter 15), do something proactive. Remember that one of the worst things you can do during times of stress is nothing. To mediate stress, we take action. Spend time around positive, uplifting people or go for a walk or call a friend or spend some time being grateful. One of our favorite proactive measures – have lunch with kids. They have a way of putting things into perspective.

◆ *MBWA* – This acronym was popularized in the 1970s and 1980s as a management technique. It stands for *managing by walking around*. It's basically a reminder to be visible and attentive to your staff. When they see us "in the trenches" by doing playground duty and helping out during dismissal and by spending time in classrooms, it builds trust.

◆ *Review Chapter 3* – Much of the ideas we share here are based on the assumption that a work-life balance is also a priority for you. Now might be a good time to go back and review Chapter 3 to remind yourself of some of those key ideas.

◆ *Preview Chapter 18* – In that chapter we talk about the need to forgive (and be forgiven) and to apologize when necessary. As you read that chapter, keep in mind what we discussed about the foundational importance of relationships.

◆ *Simplify* – Relationships, at their core, require two things: time and knowledge. Well, they actually require much more than those two things, but without them, relationships are impossible. So think in terms of who you need to find out more about (gather some knowledge) and who you need to spend time with. After all, you can spend lots of time with someone but not know anything about them and the relationship will be shallow. Likewise, you can know a lot about someone but not spend any time with them and the bond is also shallow. But when you spend time with someone and you know some things about them, the relationship can flourish.

8

Resilient School Leaders – Focus on Organization

In a Nutshell ✅

Not only is disorganization personally stressful, but a disorganized leader can also wreak havoc on an organization. Resilient leaders strive to be organized in their communication methods, daily work habits, and workspace.

Digging Deeper 🔍

We all heard it growing up, "It's time to clean your room." For many of us, that weekly (sometimes daily) reminder was a needed spark of motivation in order to get us moving. For some of you, it may have been followed by an "or else" reminder of what happens if you don't clean your room. The admonition to clean your room wasn't just about making sure nothing was growing a fungus or about making sure you had clean clothes. Our parents knew that a clean, organized, and orderly environment was good for our overall well-being.

DOI: 10.4324/9781003301356-8

Now that we are adults, we are in charge of our own environment. We no longer have those weekly reminders or parents nagging us until the task is complete. But our space says a lot about us. The way we organize our physical space (our offices, our common areas, etc.) is form of communication. Have you ever thought about it that way before? Organization of space, materials, furniture, etc. is a powerful form of communication. If our physical spaces (literally – the way we organize them) are communicating, have you considered what those spaces are saying? Organization matters. You probably don't need to be convinced of that by way of research and evidence, but we'll offer just a bit anyway.

Organization is related to our mental state. When we are organized, we feel a sense of accomplishment, our productivity improves, and are more efficient with our time (Sander, 2019). In organized environments, we can spend our time focusing on what really matters. On the other hand, when we are disorganized our stress and impulsivity increases (Chae and Rui, 2014). Working or living in a disorderly environment threatens our sense of personal control. Quite simply, cluttered and disorganized environments increase our stress levels (Sander et al., 2019).

If research doesn't convince you, your personal experience probably does. Have you ever entered a business, for example, that didn't seem to have their act together? The lobby area was cluttered, disorganized, or dirty. Or, it may have been a bit shabby or dated in its décor. The people may have been great, but the surroundings weren't. Those surroundings probably made you a bit cautious, more aware, or even distrustful. In essence, the wrong environment puts us on edge. The right environment allows us to relax and helps to instill confidence.

Being organized is one of those things that must be cultivated. Just as resiliency comes from the repeated practice of effective habits (Hanson & Hanson, 2020), so does the practice of organizational habits. Resilient leaders manage what they can control and pay attention to the environment. Don't just take advantage of those "scheduled" times to spring clean or declutter. Instead, get into the habit of daily or weekly considering those organizational strategies that may help you to be a more effective leader.

You already know the price of disorganization – decreased productivity, distrust from staff and parents, personal frustration, lack of sleep, etc. The opposite is also true – when we are organized, our stress levels decrease, we can get more done, and we love our jobs.

For our purposes here, think of organization in three broad categories. The suggestions and Application Points listed below will fall into one of these three categories.

◆ *Physical spaces* – Consider the state of the offices, meeting rooms, hallways, classrooms, cafeterias, and playgrounds, etc. As teachers and leaders, we sometimes get frustrated that students don't take good care of their surroundings. Sometimes they write on things that shouldn't be written on, they litter, they destroy, or vandalize. Or perhaps they're just messy. But consider if the adults in your building also exhibit the same behaviors. Students will only take care of their spaces to the extent that the adults do. Are the classrooms cluttered and disorganized? Are the hallways littered and messy? Are the bathrooms clean and comfortable? Remember that organization is communication. Consider what those areas are communicating to students, staff, and visitors.

◆ *Documents and papers (both physical and electronic)* – Consider how you organize and keep track of the sheer amount of information coming your way on a daily basis. Much of that information is in the form of paper. How do you keep track of it all? Most of us fall into one of two categories when it comes to dealing with papers, notes, handouts, binders, and copies – you are either a "piler" or a "filer". You either place those papers in a pile (with the hope of finding it again in the future when it's needed) or a "filer"; you file papers away into folders, notebooks, and file cabinets. Regardless, everyone needs a system.

◆ *Calendar/time* – We all need a good system to keep track of our meetings, deadlines, due dates, and action items. Are you organized when it comes to keeping track of important meetings and deadlines? Are you always running late because you forgot something? Missing deadlines or arriving late to appointments is extremely stressful. We'll dive into this topic more in the next chapter, but for now, consider how well you are organizing your time.

Application Points

- ◆ *Use organizational tools* – There are many electronic organizational apps available these days. Whether you want to create checklists, plan your time, or track your habits, there's an app for that. Take the time to find the tool that is right for you and use it with fidelity.
- ◆ *Schedule your daily tasks* – Educator, author, and international speaker LaVonna Roth frequently refers to the saying, "What gets scheduled, gets done." She encourages others to consistently *schedule time for scheduling your time*. Whether time is scheduled every week, month, or quarter, set aside time to literally schedule everything out. This includes bedtime, the time it takes to get ready in the mornings, driving time, exercise, work … you get the idea. Then, step back and take a look at your schedule. Make sure there is balance between personal time and work time (revisit Chapter 3 if you need a reminder).
- ◆ *Adapt to your environment* – Different things work for different people at different times, so adjustments may be needed. There are going to be times when the schedule is jampacked with meetings, holiday events, or just off-campus expectations that limit time during the week. In these situations, focus on one thing to stay on top off. Remember, it's about paying attention to what you can control.
- ◆ *Write it down* – Always relying on memory to recall important items is setting yourself up for failure. No matter what age, our memory fails at times. This is especially true when we have too much information to absorb or are feeling overloaded. Get in the habit of carrying

something with you (pen/paper, cell phone) and take the time to write down important tasks and reminders. This written list can become a checklist to see what you have accomplished for the day or reframed to be a "victory list" where you can celebrate the completion of important tasks.

◆ *Create a "home" base with clearly defined labels* – Whether you like to work with electronic information or tangible items, find a special place where the information or items always go. This will help alleviate stress and reduce the time it takes to locate the item when it's needed. After all, you've likely experienced the panic and frustration when you could not find where you placed or saved a document. This could look like a physical space in an office where designated shelves or cabinets hold the frequently used materials. Or with electronic documents, use a color-coded system to organize work into topics. No matter the system used, be consistent. It will ultimately keep save time and frustration.

◆ *Add yourself to your to-do list* – If you are like us, you carry with you a checklist of tasks to complete. Add yourself to that list to create the time for gratitude and reflection, time for solitude, time to unplug, etc.

◆ *Close your office door* – Your office has a door for a reason. Yes, you want to be available to staff when they need your assistance, but it is OK to occasionally close your door in order to complete important tasks. If your door is always open, you'll get the "You got a minute?" question dozens of times per day. It's hard to get into a flow and complete work when there are constant interruptions.

◆ *Do a campus walk* – Invite a friend or a colleague, someone who doesn't spend a lot of time on your campus, to do a campus walk with you. Ask for their view and perspective on how the physical environment is organized. Ask things like, "What is visually distracting?" or "What might be unappealing?" It's important to get a different perspective on your campus/building because you've likely become blind to the environment. There are some things that you may not even "see" anymore because you've seen them so many times.

◆ *Avoid the excuses* – Your campus might be old. We get that. Not all of us have the opportunity to work in brand new buildings. Your campus might not have tons of storage. We get that, too. Or the color scheme and furniture might be right out the 1970s (burnt orange carpets and lime green countertops, anyone?). All those things might be valid, but it does not mean we can't make the best use of what we have.

◆ *Start now* – Now is the time to focus on organization. Start small, pick one thing, and be consistent. Maybe that means before leaving work each night, your desk gets straightened up, or picking one small area each week in your workspace to declutter. Don't forget to add this time to the calendar.

9

Resilient School Leaders – Protect Their Time

In a Nutshell ✓

You only have so much of it and you cannot do everything. As a leader, there are more demands on your time than is reasonable or do-able. Resilient school leaders have a plan and are proactive about how they spend their time.

Digging Deeper 🔍

Life is a juggling act. In fact, that image – a circus juggler – is a great analogy for being a school leader. At any given moment you've got many balls in the air. There are times when you are juggling and balancing everything just fine and then ... *wham* – someone throws a few more balls in the mix and you frantically try to keep everything from falling to the ground. We'll admit, maybe that's an extreme analogy. But we're willing to bet there are at least a few times during the school year when you feel like one false move and everything will unravel.

DOI: 10.4324/9781003301356-9

Before we get to the Application Points, we want to dig into just one very important idea – attempting to multitask is actually working against you and adding to your stress. Here is the big idea – stop trying to multitask. Why? Because it's impossible. You cannot multitask. Let's repeat that – multitasking is not possible; it's a myth.

We understand why there's a temptation to attempt it. You have more to accomplish and more to get done that you have time in the day. This is especially true if you are taking our advice to *strive for a work-life balance* and *prioritize relationships* and *put your mask on first.* You might be thinking, "*If I'm going to do all these things and run my school, I have to multitask.*" Again, we understand the mentality. We've fallen victim to it as well. In fact, one of us got a less-than-great annual evaluation from a supervisor and told "You need to do a better job of multitasking."

Before we proceed, we should probably define it: multitasking is attempting to complete more than one cognitive task at a time. Multitasking, the way we are discussing it, is not defined as doing more than one thing at a time. We do more than one thing at a time every day. We can eat lunch and answer emails simultaneously. We can walk and have a discussion at the same time. We can even mindlessly listen to music while driving. But in each of those examples, only one of them requires our focus and attention. Cognitively it's not possible to do more than one thing at a time. It's related to our attention and focus. You can only focus and attend to one thing at a time. Fabritius and Hageman, in their outstanding book titled *The Leading Brain* (2017) put it this way, attempting to multitask is the "archenemy of focus."

Here's the real-world definition of multitasking: screwing up several things simultaneously. A real-life example may help to elaborate on this truth. Imagine you are at your desk drafting a memo that will go to staff regarding a procedural change in the school schedule. It's an important memo. You are working hard to make sure it's clear and you're doing your best to anticipate questions and reactions. This memo requires your full devotion and attention. In the middle of drafting that memo, your email chimes and you see a message from the superintendent. You stop what you're doing to read that email.

Think about what happens in that scenario. You are not simultaneously writing a memo and reading the email. You are not multitasking; you are task switching. You might be thinking, *"Yeah. That sounds right. What's wrong with that?"* As highlighted in the bestselling book *Brain Rules* (2008) Dr. John Medina points out that task-switching (which some people misconstrue as multitasking) actually results in cognitive loss. In other words, every time you switch from one cognitive task to another, there is a loss in cognitive energy and focus.

Consider again that scenario with the superintendent's email. This is likely what happens – you are working hard at drafting the memo to staff. It's got your focus and attention. You halt that focus and attention in order to read the email. Once you've read that email and it's time to switch tasks back to the memo, you've lost some of your thoughts and ideas. In essence, that interruption (that switching of tasks) stymied the groove you were in. When it's time to switch from reading the email back to drafting the memo in some ways you have to start all over again. You likely say something, *"OK. Now where was I?"* And this *"Where was I?"* process takes additional time, adds additional cognitive demand, and ultimately makes you less productive.

What's our take-away? When you have something important to focus on – something that needs your undivided attention – focus solely on that thing and remove other possible interruptions. In our scenario, that means shutting down email, closing the office door, turning off your phone, and telling the office staff to only interrupt you in case of an emergency. In other words, you are better off focusing on just the one thing. Protect your time and your emotional energy by avoiding the temptation to multitask. In the long run, you'll be more productive and produce better outcomes when your focus is undivided.

Application Points

- *Remember to say "no"* – Here's that suggestion again: be careful about what you say yes and no to. Saying yes to too

many things – taking on too many unnecessary responsibilities – only adds to your stress levels. In the case of
multitasking and meeting the needs of your staff, sometimes the "no" is *"I want to help, but I can't do it right now."*

◆ *Think of time as a system* – Have you heard the saying,
"Every system is perfectly designed to get the results it
gets?" Time is a system. If you are not getting the results
you want, change the system. And remember what Zig
Ziglar (1975), said in *See You at the Top*, "People often complain about a lack of time when the lack of direction is the
real problem."

◆ *Close the office door* – We've all heard it a million times,
"Hey, you got a quick minute?" Rarely is the conversation
a quick minute and those conversations almost always
interrupt something you are doing (not to mention the
conversation probably results in something added to
your to-do list). When you need to focus on something
important, close the office door. Having an open-door
policy does not mean that the door is literally always
open. It means that you are available and willing to
engage with staff.

◆ *Reward yourself* – When you have a difficult task (or one
that you simply try to avoid), schedule something fun,
interesting, or interactive as a reward for completing that
less-than-desirable task. Say to yourself, *"Once I get this
done, I get to _____."* or *"As a reward for getting this done,
I am going to …."*

◆ *Challenge the "first in, last out" mentality* – It's true, you
need to be visible and spend lots of time on the school
grounds. But if you adopt the *"I've always got to be there,
sun up to sun down"* mentality, you are on the quick road
to burnout. Speaking of burnout, you might want to
jump ahead to Chapter 12. We have some good thoughts
on how to recognize and combat burnout.

◆ *Remember Parkinson's law* – Parkinson's law is the idea
that the work we have will expand to fill the time we've
allotted for its completion. The idea was first espoused
by Cyril Northcote Parkinson in an essay he wrote for

The Economist in 1955. He was attempting to be humorous but many of us have found that law to be unfortunately true. Schedules, plans, goals, and deadlines will help to increase productivity.

◆ *Speaking of schedules* – Start your day with a preview of your calendar. Consider the meetings and tasks you need to complete and create a plan to complete them. If you are fortunate enough to have administrative support, schedule a time each week to sit down with your assistant to talk through the week's schedule of events.

◆ *Speaking of schedules, part 2* – Include time in your weekly schedule for taking care of yourself (putting your mask on) and for relationships and for gratitude and all the other things that you know are important for a balanced life.

◆ *Increase the margin* – Margin is defined as the space between capacity and demand. Consider, for example, the margin in your finances. If you have more income that outgo, you've got some margin. In relation to time, if there is no margin, you'll feel rushed and overwhelmed. Build in times for breaks, meals, and time to rest and play and occasionally – don't schedule anything at all.

◆ *Schedule time to read* – Everyone's favorite horror novelist Stephen King famously once said, "If you don't have time to read, you don't have the time to write." We'll adopt that assumption but with a small twist – "If you don't have the time to read, you don't have the time to lead." Our profession is ever-changing (as it should be) and there are new studies, new research, and new ideas coming our way every week. While no one can stay on top of everything, we do ourselves a disservice when we don't schedule the time to read professional journals, articles, and books.

◆ *"But, I'm not really a reader"* – OK, we get it. Some people like to read more than others. But reading and learning are central to leadership. Michael Fullan (2008) reminds us that "learning is the work."

◆ *"But I don't have time to read"* – Actually, you probably do have time to read. Let's do some quick math. Assuming you are an average reader (you can read about 300 words per minute) and you devote just 30 minutes a day to reading, you'll end up reading over 30 books per year. Here's the math: Average book length = 100,000 words. You can read 300 words per minute so it will take you about 333 minutes to read an average book. If you read for 30 minutes per day that's 10,950 minutes. 10,950/333 = 32 +/– books.

◆ *Understand the importance of "now"* – While it is important to learn from the past and plan for the future, all we really have is the present moment, the now. Take time to reflect, appreciate, and acknowledge what is present in your life, what is good. And make time for those things.

◆ *Don't wish for more time* – More time is not the answer. We've all thought it – "If I only had more time." Time isn't the problem. After all, there are people who have the same exact amount of time that you do but they seem to be living balanced, healthy lives. And, if we are honest, if we did have more time, would we use it wisely?

◆ *Reflect* – We spoke a bit about the need to reflect in Chapter 5 – Resilient Leaders Are Self-Aware. But it's good to remind ourselves that reflection, as a consistent habit, is necessary for learning and growth. Part of protecting your time should be focused on reflection. Consider what Henry Mintzberg said in his 2004 book *Managers not MBAs* – "Learning is not doing; it is reflecting on doing."

◆ *Don't confuse busyness with productivity or effectiveness* – We're reminded of a bumper sticker that got a good laugh, "Jesus is coming. Quick – look busy." We can be busy all day but ineffective. Phil Dobson, author of *The Brain Book* (2016) describes the differences between busyness, productivity, and effectiveness: Busyness is continually working but getting little done. Productivity is getting lots done, but not necessarily the important things. Effectiveness is spending the right amount of energy on the right things. Tim Ferriss, author of the *4-Hour Work Week* (2009) says "Slow down and remember this: most things make no difference. Being busy is a form of mental laziness."

◆ *Do a digital detox* – Step away from your devices for specific periods of time. Regarding devices ask yourself – *to or from*? Does the device or app or tool connect me *to* important tasks and people or take me away *from* them? Some people refer to a "phast" – fasting (as in abstaining) from your phone for periods of time.

10

Resilient School Leaders – Constantly Refine Communication

In a Nutshell ✓

Ineffective communication skills or practices stresses out everyone. As leaders and influencers, our job is to guide and lead people; we do so most effectively and positively when build, refine, and implement effective methods of communication.

Digging Deeper 🔍

Do a quick internet search for books focused on effective communication skills and you'll find thousands (literally thousands) of tomes devoted to the topic of communication. Do a further search for videos, articles, and blogs related to communication skills for school leaders and you'll soon be lost down a rabbit's hole of internet answers and suggestions to every conceivable topic, scenario, and situation. Because the topic is so vast (and our space here is so limited) what we'll provide is a brief overview of just a few important concepts to keep in mind as we connect the dots between stress and communication.

DOI: 10.4324/9781003301356-10

Communication is really about meaning. Or, more directly, it's about transference of meaning between groups. It's about imparting the meaning of a message and ensuring that the meaning (not just the words) are understood by the other party. When communicating, regardless of the format, the goal is a shared understanding of the meaning of the message. Conflict can be the result of inartful, ineffective, or confusing messages.

What we say matters. How we say it probably matters more. Communication involves the nuances of word choice, timing, non-verbal communication, and a whole host of other factors. Effective leaders understand that the art of communication requires proficiency (if not mastery) of these elements and they constantly work to improve what they say and how they say it. In addition, check your assumptions. Never assume that because you told someone something that they understood it to the degree necessary to act (or change thinking). Just as in teaching, we don't assume that students learned something simply because we taught it. Don't assume that because staff have been told something, that they understand it to the depth necessary to change, adapt, or assimilate.

Much of our communication is in the form of providing feedback, direction, and guidance to staff, students, and families. When providing feedback, effective leaders know that it must be direct, kind, and actionable. That last requirement is of utmost importance. Effective feedback is actionable. That is, there must be something specific that the person on the receiving of the feedback can do with the information. Vague feedback (e.g., telling a student that they need to improve their behavior or telling a staff member that they have a negative attitude) is stressful, confusing, and often results in an argument. Stress is actually reduced when feedback includes specific steps that an individual can take to improve some aspect of their lives.

While we are talking about feedback, let's briefly address the differences between a critique a criticism. If you've never considered the differences before, they are simple yet profound – particularly for school leaders. First, take a moment to do a thought experiment. Create a T-chart. On the top left of the

T-chart write the word *critique* and on the top right write the word *criticize*. Categorize the following words and phrases into one of those two categories: *subjective, objective, specific, vague, observes a behavior, judges a behavior, driven by hierarchy, driven by relationship, usually delivered in a calm manner, often delivered in a frustrated tone, goal is to inform, goal is to guilt or shame, looks to find fault, looks to find support, focuses on the deed, focuses on the person.*

If you took the time to complete the exercise above, you likely saw a pattern emerging. While we often think of them as synonyms, a critique is far different than a criticism. A critique is something that is often delivered by an expert. Think, for example, of a food critic. A qualified and valid critic is one who has expertise, training, and background in the discipline they are evaluating. Their expertise is the foundation of the critique, and it focuses on an examination or evaluation of a product or outcome. In other words, it's not personal. A dictionary definition might use the phrase "a detailed analysis" or "an assessment" of a situation, outcome, or product. A critique includes both a discussion of positive outcomes and areas for improvement.

A criticism, on the other hand, is typically a negative statement of disapproval often focused on the person rather than the behavior or outcome. A dictionary definition might include "an expression of disapproval" and "focused on finding fault." For our purposes here, the key thing to remember is that if we want to help people grow and improve, understanding the differences is essential. When our focus is criticism, relationships suffer and stress increases. But when we strive to remove the personal and stay focused on outcomes, it's better for everyone. The sorting exercise above, by the way, comes from our friend and colleague Shauna King (www.shaunafking.com). She has done great work in helping educators understand the nature and importance of effective communication skills and we highly suggest you check out her work.

One final note – leadership, at its very essence – is communication. We can't effectively lead without the ability to effectively communicate. When we unartfully or outright ineffectively communicate with those we lead, our effectiveness is limited or null.

Application Points

- *Proofread everything* – Not just your *own* emails, newsletters, website updates, etc., but make sure that all written communication coming from your school or office is proofed for CUPS (capitalization, usage, punctuation, and spelling). Does this take time? Sure does. But it takes more time to clarify, apologize, or correct poorly worded messages.
- *Remember the limitations of emails and memos* – Let's set aside the frustration that some of our staff simply don't read the emails and memos that we do send out. As leaders, we were not hired to lead via memo. Memos and emails are often used to communicate directives and "must dos." No doubt, there are times when we need to provide direction and let staff know what to do. We're not suggesting that written directives are a bad thing. But keep in mind that directives may get compliance, but rarely do they result in full buy-in or commitment. To get the kind of dedication and commitment we need to ensure change, we need to be with people. Noting replaces good ol' fashioned face time.
- *Reply, reply all, CC, or BCC?* – Never hit "reply all" in an email message unless you really mean to. While you probably should not be delivering or communicating sensitive or confidential information via email anyway, it's a recipe for conflict and confusion when people are included in a message when they should not be. The same goes for who you choose to include in the message (cc or bcc).
- *Take your time crafting messages* – When it comes to things like communicating a new vision for your school or considering how to get staff on board for a new initiative, take time to consider how to deliver the message. Specific words and phrases, the timing of the message, and who delivers the message are important. A rushed message is

often a confusing or incomplete one. The right words at the right time can get great results. The wrong words at the wrong time can turn a bad situation into a nightmare. But, the right words at the wrong time may also backfire. It's a delicate dance. Best-selling author and leadership guru Max DePree (2004) reminds us that muddy, imprecise language will result in muddy, imprecise thinking on the part of our audience

◆ *Ask yourself, "Do I understand my own message?"* – As strange as this may sound, it's actually a really important habit to practice. We sometimes don't understand something as well as we think we do. In addition, if your message was primarily drafted, refined, and "discussed" only in your own mind, when it comes time to verbally explain that idea, it can fall apart.

◆ *Then filter, a lot* – Resilient leaders don't always say what they think. They have an active filter that takes out many of the words, phrases, explanations, and examples that they may want to use. A powerful message is a simple one. If, for example, you've written a memo or email that outlines a new procedure, do your best to remove all unnecessary references, words, or examples that may confuse the main message. Value people's time by being concise – particularly in written communications. The sad fact is that people don't read long email messages.

◆ *Give out handwritten notes of appreciation and encouragement* – Effective school leaders are tremendously appreciative of the big and little things that staff, students, and parents do on a daily basis. In fact, we are probably more appreciative than they realize. When we take opportunities to express that appreciation via handwritten thank you notes, everyone wins.

◆ *Open meetings with appreciations* – Particularly during times of uncertainty and high stress for staff, start off meetings with gratitude and appreciations. Make sharing them a part of the DNA of your organization. When people feel appreciated and noticed, they'll be more open to tackling tough issues.

◆ *Avoid highlighting what you don't have* – For example, when talking with prospective teachers or staff, focus on what the school has to offer instead of what it is lacking. Avoid saying things like, "Well, our technology is out of date" or "We don't get a lot of parent support or participation here." Instead say things like, "We've made a commitment to updating our technology and the plan we've put together for the next year is impressive" and "The parents that participate and get involved here are committed to doing what is best for our students." This simple shift in language can make a big difference.

◆ *Remove pronouns* – This suggestion appears also in Chapter 14 Resilient School Leaders Become Experts in Conflict. The removal of terms like *I, they, you, we,* and *them* is important, particularly during times of change or conflict. When we use pronouns, we make things personal. When things are personal, we risk the message coming across more as a criticism than a critique.

◆ *Learn about social proof* – You may never have heard of this concept, but you likely experience it on a daily basis. It is the tendency for our behavior (everyone's behavior, even your own) to be highly influenced by other people. And it actually runs your organization. For example, if someone you know and trust and says, "I just read the most amazing book. It changed my life!" you are influenced or biased towards reading that book. If a group of friends tells you that a movie they saw wasn't worth the cost of the ticket, you think twice about seeing it yourself. If everyone else is driving 15 mph over the speed limit, you tend to go with the flow of traffic. In essence, we are influenced by those around us. We are influenced by their words and their actions. This can be good or bad, of course. When it comes to communication, how we talk about the challenges at our school matters in how people will think about them. If we say, "We have way too many students coming late to class" that will make it appear to be a significant problem when it actually might not be. In that case, we are highlighting the negative behavior of a few students. But if we say, "At our school, 95% of the students arrive to class on time, ready to learn" that shifts the focus; it shifts the social proof from the negative to the positive.

11

Resilient School Leaders – Listen

In a Nutshell ✅

Listening, effective listening that is, is a foundational skill for all school leaders. When we are good at listening to those we lead, it reduces not only our own stress levels but the stressors experienced by our staff.

Digging Deeper 🔍

There is much written, in both popular literature and research-driven journals, about the need for leaders to be good at listening to others. For our purposes here, we won't attempt a review of that literature. You likely already know some of what we might include in that review (listening is an active process, for example) and you've no doubt attended a leadership workshop or two that included listening as a topic of discussion. What we'll do here is provide an insight into a topic you may never have connected to the art of listening: *the brain's default habits.*

Something we (both Janet and Bryan) share in common is a fascination with how the brain functions. We hope you are similarly fascinated (or at least somewhat interested) in learning

DOI: 10.4324/9781003301356-11

more about some of the underlying mechanisms of the brain. For our purposes here, we'll address just one of those underlying mechanisms and then make a connection to stress and resilience. That underlying mechanism is the concept of two different kinds of thinking systems in your brain.

Daniel Kahneman, author of *Thinking, Fast and Slow* (2013), highlights an interesting and sometimes conflicting process in our ways of thinking. Most of us like to consider ourselves as thoughtful, reflective, and considerate thinkers. That is, when faced with a problem, we take the time to carefully consider options, alternatives, and solutions. We consider the unique characteristics of the issue in front of us come to a conclusion based on a thoughtful response. But, that actually happens less than we like to think. We are creatures of habit and we often respond from memory or past experience more than a careful consideration of the issue in front of us.

Dr. Kahneman describes two systems running your brain – one fast (System 1) and one slow (System 2). System 1 is fast, automatic, intuitive, and unconscious. It's what we do and how we respond to the routine, the normal, the everyday situations we face. It consists of our habits, our history, our memory, and our sometimes snap judgements about what is taking place. System 2 is slow, deliberate, attentive, and conscious. It requires that we carefully consider the unique situation in front us in order to determine the most appropriate response.

These two operating systems are essentially guides for making decisions. It makes sense, if you think about it, that our brains have these two distinct systems. Some situations don't require much in-depth thought and reflection. Others do. Let's use System 2 for a moment to dig into this idea. It takes effort, time, and it's difficult to think critically and uniquely about every problem you face. And, many of the problems you face on a daily basis are ones you faced in the past. So, we rely on memory and intuitive historical responses. That actually works well much of the time. Except when it doesn't.

Many situations, especially those that involve the need to listen carefully to people (because every person is unique), require that we use System 2; that we slow down and be mindful (shameless reference to Chapter 6). In the book Dr. Kahneman invites the reader on an investigation of the rational mind and the process of rational thinking. We like to think of ourselves as rational, thoughtful, and reflective most of the time. In actuality, much of the time we are fast and responsive in our thinking.

These two operating systems are necessary, of course, and each play an important role. For our discussion here, the essential take aways are: (1) Be aware that these two systems exist; (2) Be aware that sometimes you respond with System 1 when you should respond with System 2; and (3) Every person you lead is expecting you to respond with System 2. And, we might add, each person you lead deserves a slow, thoughtful response to something that they believe is important.

Here is a connection to stress in case you haven't made it already – when we are stressed we tend to rely on System 1. It makes sense. System 1 is fast and we can deal with the issue quickly and then go on to the next. Again, this system works just fine for normal and routine problems. Except when it doesn't. We've all made those mistakes in leadership – you came to a quick decision about something only to find out later that there was more to the story and more information that need to be considered. When that happens, your stress levels increase.

Application Points

- ◆ *Conduct entry interviews* – These are formal, structured, but short meetings with all staff when are new to a building or school. You simply take a few minutes to meet privately with each staff member (from the teacher with the most seniority to the custodial staff) in order to seek their perspectives, ideas, and hopes for the school. Your job is to listen and find out people's stories and histories.
- ◆ *Consider why people repeat things* – You have people on your staff who tend to repeat or re-hash the same hurts, offenses, or pet peeves over and over. Have you ever wondered why they do that? Most people tend to get repetitive when they don't feel heard or listened to. In all

reality, some people *are* listened to, but they still bring up past offenses repeatedly, and they probably need some serious counseling. In those situations when reasonable and hard-working people bring up issues again and again, it's because they don't feel like they've been heard. In those cases, try this – say, " I'm not sure I am listening like I should have because you've shared this story again. What am I not understanding?"

◆ *Adopt a servant mentality* – Servants listen. Robert Greenleaf, the author of the highly respected classic work titled *Servant Leadership* (1977) said this decades ago, "Only a true natural servant automatically responds to any problem by listening first." This aligns well (but predated) Stephen Covey's advice to *seek first to understand, then to be understood*.

◆ *Re-read Stephen Covey* – He popularized the saying, "Seek first to understand, then to be understood". Of all of Stephen Covey's excellent reminders of the habits of effective people, this one stands out to us as perhaps the most important. Essentially, we need to remember that listening with the goal of truly understanding someone's perspective is essential for all aspects of school leadership. Lousy listeners make lousy leaders. And, as you've hopefully connected already, when any aspect of leadership is ineffective, stress increases. If it's been a while since you've read *The 7 Habits of Highly Effective People*, put it at the top of your reading list.

◆ *Seek feedback from staff* – Offer your staff an opportunity to provide feedback about your leadership skills and practices. Twice per year give your staff an anonymous survey seeking input into your skills, strengths, and areas for improvement. This takes tremendous vulnerability, of course, because some staff will take the opportunity to be unnecessarily critical. Sometimes they'll be outright mean and offensive. But it's necessary to both gather and act upon feedback, and it models exactly what you are asking of them when you complete their annual evaluation.

◆ *Seek feedback from a mentor* – Ask a mentor or a trusted colleague this question, "Do I exhibit any negative, off putting, or odd ticks or quirks that signal that I'm not listening?" Or ask, "What characteristics do I demonstrate that I am listening?"

◆ *Empathize* – This is easier for some of us than it is for others. Empathy can be defined as *compassion in action.* Recall that stress is managed by taking control. Empathy actually helps to take some control by taking some action.

◆ *Prepare for messiness* – Just because we actively and intentionally listen to someone does not mean that we'll (1) Understand what they mean or (2) Agree with them. Bob Sutton, organizational psychologist at Stanford University, and author of numerous books including *Good Boss, Bad Boss* (2012) says that saying smart things and giving smart answers are important. Learning to listen to others and asking smart questions is more important. He also says to strive for simplicity and competence but embrace the confusion and messiness along the way.

◆ *Ask probing, open ended questions* – Max DePree in *Leadership is an Art* (2004) reminds us that listening is "more than a mechanical exchange of information." It involves nuance, hidden meanings, and often uses the same words to communicate different ideas. When listening, ask questions such as, "Tell me more about ...", "I'm curious how ..." or "Could you provide an example of ..."

◆ *Paraphrase* – Just about every suggestion focused on how to improve listening skills includes some aspect of a paraphrase. They are powerful and important. But, we'll suggest that you don't say, "What I hear you saying is ...". That phrase is overused and can sometime come across as trite or even sarcastic. And, it might actually be a System 1 response. Instead say something like, "This is the issue ... Am I right?" or "The most important thing is ... Do I understand that correctly?"

◆ *Take your time* – Some decisions and scenarios require time to consider an appropriate response. Don't be shy about taking the time needed to carefully engage System

2. You might respond to someone by saying, "This is an important issue. I'm going to take some time to think about it." In classrooms, we tell teachers to allow for think time/wait time so that students can formulate thoughtful and accurate answers to our questions. The same goes for us.

◆ *Remove pronouns* – This suggestion appears in Chapter 14's discussion of conflict as well. During difficult or emotionally laden conversations, remove pronouns (references to groups and individuals) and focus on the issues. Instead of saying something like, "I see you are mad about ____ because we ..." say, "The issue that needs to be discussed is ...". Removing pronouns can help to lower the "emotional" temperature of the discussion.

◆ *Prepare for gossip* – People gossip. That's an unfortunate truth. When you adopt an open stance where you are willing to listen to people, they'll sometimes gossip and complain about others. Be prepared and have a pat, routine, and practiced response when gossip is coming your way. Obviously, don't engage in the gossip, but be ready to put an end to it when it comes your way.

◆ *Don't try to multitask* – A refresher about the discussion in Chapter 9 might be a good idea. Go back and remind yourself of the risk of trying to multitask and then make connections to the importance of listening.

◆ *Come back to this chapter* – After you've read Chapter 13 (change) and Chapter 14 (conflict) come back to this chapter to connect the dots. In all reality, we could have placed the information about System 1 and System 2 in either of those chapters. Our thinking patterns and decision-making systems impact how we'll respond during times of change and conflict.

12

Resilient School Leaders – Recognize and Combat Burnout

In a Nutshell ✅

There is a limit, regardless of how resilient you already are, to how much you can handle. If you burn out, everyone suffers. The good news is that the signs of burnout can be recognized and there are specific steps you can take to prevent it.

Digging Deeper 🔍

We've all had those days when we feel overly tired, disillusioned, overwhelmed by the work, and a bit cranky. Whether those days are a sign of pending doom or not remains to be seen. But, burnout is a real thing. In fact, in 2019, the World Health Organization (WHO) recognized burnout as a disease. You read that correctly. Burnout is a recognizable, diagnosable, and treatable disease.

So then, what is burnout? The WHO defines burnout as a phenomenon resulting from "workplace stress that has not been successfully managed." The key idea here is the "not successfully

DOI: 10.4324/9781003301356-12

managed" part. As we've discussed, exposure to stress is not really the problem. The problem is the inability to successfully manage the stress we have.

At is simplest, we can think of burnout as unrelieved stress. Pierce Howard, in his 2006 encyclopedic book *The Owner's Manual for the Brain*, puts it this way:

> Burnout occurs after one or more stressors continue their obstruction and unrelenting intensity and effectiveness; the individual feels out of control over an extended time and eventually gives up hope of eliminating or even reducing the effect of the stressor.

That unrelieved stress and feeling that too many factors are beyond your control, over time, leads to burnout. And when we feel burned out, it's hard to get up and go to work in the morning.

In the early 1980s, researcher Christina Maslach and her colleagues developed the Maslach Burnout Inventory (MBI) in order to help organizations gather data about the stressors and challenges that impact workplace productivity and overall employee health. The MBI contains three dimensions of burnout: exhaustion, cynicism, and professional efficacy.

These three dimensions offer a view of how burnout manifests itself and offers us a way to think about it in concrete, measurable terms. It is important to note that the MBI is not designed to determine an *individual's* level of personal burnout. There is not specific point at which the MBI data determines that a person is burned out or not. Some organizations have attempted to do that very thing; they ask employees to take the MBI in order to determine who is burned out, who is about to burn out, and which ones are managing their stress effectively. Dr. Maslach calls this a misuse of the MBI. It is designed to be a data-collecting tool to help organizations analyze factors that impact employee well-being. Since the first use of the MBI, it has undergone several revisions, but the data collected over the years points to some interesting insights that we can use to do a bit of self-reflection. Here are a few key insights from Dr. Maslach and others who have done research on this topic:

◆ As a result of the pandemic, the teacher shortage, and other factors, nearly half of school principals report being overwhelmed and on the edge of burnout (Steiner et al., 2022).

◆ When compared to the general population, school leaders report more difficulty sleeping and are at a greater risk of depression (Robinson, 2018).

◆ High performers, even those who like their jobs, can still burn out (Moss, 2020).

◆ Individuals in purpose-driven work are still susceptible to burnout (Whiteside, 2018).

◆ In some occupations (including education) the norm is to put others' needs first. In such occupations, when combined with a lack of resources and support, burnout becomes a relevant and significant issue (Maslach & Leiter, 2016).

◆ Regardless of how good you are, you cannot do it all (D'Sousa, 2021). What you elect *not* to do might be just as important as what you elect to do. The first Application Point below will remind you of the power of saying "no."

◆ The good news – not everyone gets burned out even when faced with difficult, long-term challenges. You can learn to thrive during less-than-ideal circumstances (McKee & Wiens, 2021).

◆ Burnout is multi-causal. It includes organizational causes as well as interpersonal ones (Skovholt & Trotter-Mathison, 2016).

Admittedly, the information and statistics listed above can be a bit depressing. While our goal was not to add more worry to your life, we did want to get your attention. Burnout is a real thing and if we don't take specific steps to deal with it, well … you know how the story goes.

Burnout can be defined, quantified, and prevented assuming you know what to look for. So, what do we look for? What are the signs that we may be leaning towards burnout? While not an exhaustive list, the following reflection questions are a good place to start:

- ◆ When was the last time you had fun at your job?
- ◆ Are you able to see a connection between your daily tasks and your purpose?
- ◆ When was the last time you sought counsel, advice, and input from a mentor or trusted colleague?
- ◆ How often do you visit classrooms?
- ◆ How often do you take specific steps *to put your mask on*?
- ◆ In what ways are you practicing gratitude on a consistent basis?
- ◆ Are you helping others practice gratitude?
- ◆ Are you able to turn off the phone and unplug from social media on a consistent basis?
- ◆ What small, seemingly inconsequential things might be slowly chipping away at your ability to do your job?
- ◆ What is the biggest frustration you have at work right now?
- ◆ What is the biggest joy you have at work right now?

Application Points

- ◆ *Say no* – As we've suggested several times already, be thoughtful as to what you say "yes" to. Adding too many things to an already-packed schedule or list of responsibilities will undoubtedly increase your stress and lead to burnout.
- ◆ *Resist the urge to work more* – Working more might be a trap, not a solution. Consider the way University of Pennsylvania researchers Annie McKee and Kandi Wiens (2021) put it, "Just doing more – and more, and more – rarely fixes problems, and it usually makes things worse, because we are essentially manufacturing our own stress." Rather, a solution might be to focus your work efforts on those things that are most likely to align well with your personal purpose. Now might be a good time to review the suggestions listed in Chapter 4 Resilient School Leaders Focus on Purpose.
- ◆ *Schedule breaks during the day* – We realize that emergencies happen and being a school leader is partially defined

as dealing with the unexpected, but it is important to schedule times to pause and catch your breath. We give classroom teachers planning periods and lunch breaks. We should do the same for ourselves.

◆ *Read something interesting* – Related to the profession, what are you reading that makes you excited? What are you learning that gives you hope for the future? Our bias is this: when you stop learning, you significantly limit your ability to lead. And when we stop learning and growing and improving, burnout and cynicism are happy to take over.

◆ *Unplug* – Removing yourself from the demands and distractions of electronic devices is a must in order to manage stress. Maybe it's just for an hour at a time. Maybe for a few days during a long weekend. Regardless, regularly schedule time to step away from the digital world in order to catch your breath and recalibrate.

◆ *Seek input from a mentor* – When you have someone in your life who knows you well and will speak the truth to you, you are a rich person. Regularly meet with that person and ask them to give you feedback about how well you are handling the stressors of the job.

◆ *Develop a professional support network* – While you might be the only one in your building or organization with a specific job title, you are not the only one doing that job. Seek input, advice, and ideas from those people who do the same work.

◆ *Reflect* – Another suggestion you'll find throughout this book focuses on the need for personal reflection. For our discussion here, an important question to consider is, "*If I was burned out (or close to it), how would I know?*" Better yet, ask that question of your mentor or your professional support network.

◆ *Recognize your inner dialogue* – We all talk to ourselves; it's natural and it's human. Often referred to ask self-talk, it's the inner dialogue that takes place in our minds. Sometimes we are aware of that conversation but often-times we are not. When we experience high levels of stress, our inner dialogue quickly leans towards the negative and the critical. And it's easy to get stuck there. When you realize that your inner dialogue (the way you talk to yourself) may be too critical or negative, take specific steps to change it. You can start by taking two simple steps: First, merely name the emotion that is the focus of the self-talk. Maybe it's frustration or irritation or cynicism or outright anger. Whatever it is, name it. Then, once you've recognized that you are having a less-than-healthy internal discussion, take action. That's the second step. Answer the question, *"What can I do right now to bring this situation, issue, or emotion back into perspective?"* Perhaps you need to unplug from social media, or take a walk, or visit classrooms, or go home for the day. The key idea is that taking action is how we manage stress. We take back some control in order to lower our stress and bring our internal dialogue back to a healthier place.

◆ *Vent carefully* – When feelings of frustration or irritation get the best of us, we all need a safe place to express and release that negative energy. But we also know this, not everyone can (or should be) trusted. You need an outlet, there's no doubt about that, but resilient people are careful to vent only with people who are highly trustworthy.

◆ *But, wait. What do I do if I'm already burned out?* – The snarky and short-sighted answer to this question is – find another job. But we know that it's not always easy, practical, or feasible. The first step is to seek counsel, advice, and wisdom from those you know and trust. If you feel like you are burned out, take action. Remember that we manage stress by taking control. While you may feel stuck in your current job or position, consider what small changes or adjustments could be made in order to find more joy and energy in the work.

◆ *"I'm not yet burned out, but I am getting crispy around the edges"* – There is a cost to being a leader. Leadership taxes our emotions, our physical energy, and our spiritual centeredness. That's not necessarily a bad thing, of course. There is a cost to everything. But we become burned out when that cost becomes more than we can pay. A good place to start is by considering which aspects of the job is taxing you the most. There are five main reasons that people burn out (Wigert & Agrawal, 2018): unfair treatment, unmanageable workload, lack of role clarity, lack of communication and support from a supervisor, and unreasonable time pressure. In reference to those five areas, consider which one(s) are providing the highest level of stress, and then take action to address them.

13

Resilient School Leaders – Understand Change

In a Nutshell ✅

Change, even when self-initiated, is stressful. Effective leaders not only understand that stressors accompany change, they take specific steps to understand how change impacts they people they lead.

Digging Deeper 🔍

As leaders, we are in the change business. Perhaps said more accurately, we are in the improvement business. But, improvement requires change. So, we are in the change business.

To start, it is a bit unfair to attempt to tackle a complex topic like change in such a short chapter. While we won't attempt to do a thorough (or even adequate) review of the topic, we'll attempt to remind us of how change impacts the people we lead. We'll offer a few important notes about change as it relates to leadership, stress, and resiliency.

DOI: 10.4324/9781003301356-13

As leaders, we often get excited about new initiatives and change. For example, we may attend a summer conference and learn new instructional approaches or techniques and then proclaim to our staff, *here is what we are going to do this year*. Understandably, this can cause stress among your staff. And, as you likely already know, when stress is high, change is hard (Wisse & Sleebos, 2016).

Most of us who are drawn to leadership like, enjoy, and embrace change. Or, at the very least, we are adept at it. Many who are drawn to classroom teaching (a career of it, anyway) like and embrace continuity, consistency, and sameness. This, understandably, can cause friction between the teacher who desires consistency and the leader who wants things to change. By the way, it's important to recognize that a desire for consistency is not a bad thing. When a teacher knows what to expect year after year, they can get good (perhaps really good) at it. This is why so many teachers like to stay at the same grade level for many years. This is also why some of them struggle to implement new curricula or new initiatives. When trying new things, their self-efficacy takes a hit. When that happens, stress levels skyrocket. By the way, we don't assume that teachers don't want to change, improve, or try new things. Many of them do. The point is that change, when forced from outside sources, can be stressful and teachers and leaders often have very different perspectives.

Change can be exciting in principle but challenging in practice. When we learn new things, it is often in the abstract via a blog, a newsletter, a book, or a workshop. Those formats often focus on a theoretical base and research evidence for the effectiveness of the idea. That's good. Our educational approaches need to be based in good theory and research. But there is a huge gap between the theory we learn about in the comfort of a workshop and putting that theory into practice with real kids in real classrooms (Frey, Fisher, & Pumpian, 2012). The real work of change takes place in classrooms, not in workshops.

Additionally, leaders don't actually implement instructional change. The job of implementing instructional change is the job of the classroom teacher. As leaders, we are not actually in the classroom teaching the lessons with the new curriculum or implementing the new instructional approach. Yes, we may occasionally teach a class or fill in when needed. But, our day-to-day job is not in the classroom. By way of analogy, coaches don't actually play the game. Coaches are important, necessary, and essential but the game is played by the players.

Part of understanding and being adept at change is understanding that change is often ambiguous. *What* needs to be changed is often quite clear (graduation rates or test scores, for example) but *how* to achieve the change can be quite unclear and open to interpretation. The *what* is clear, the *how* is often not. This truth can also a source of conflict and disagreement among staff. While it may be easy to get buy-in from staff about the *what*, the *how* is what requires the hard work and effort. The *how*, if you think about it, is really the focus of the change. And when we remember that it is the staff and teachers who are implementing the change (literally, implementing the *how*), we can see why it can become a source of conflict and stress.

For a deeper dive into change, the change process, and a leader's responsibility to guide change, we'll point you to some of the excellent work done by the likes of educator Michael Fullan, Harvard researcher John Kotter, and, of course, the classic *Who Moved My Cheese?* by Spencer Johnson.

Application Points

♦ *Practice reframing* – A lot has been written about reframing including, by the way, an entire chapter in *17 Things Resilient Teachers Do* (2021). But a quick recap might be helpful. Reframing is mental talk that focuses on intentionally changing perspective and thinking about a situation. The key here is intentionality. When we reframe a situation, we elect to think about it differently. For example, the frame we might put around a piece of art does not actually change the art, it simply changes the way we view that piece of art. Likewise, when dealing with change, be intentional about the way you think about the situation in front of you. This is especially important when the change is mandated rather than by choice. Shawn Achor, author of *The Happiness Advantage* (2018), puts it this way, "It's not necessarily the reality that shapes us but the lens through which your brain views the world that shapes your reality."

◆ *Use phrases of influence* – Phil Jones (2017) suggests that there are phrases and statements that can effectively influence people to change. Among them are:

- "I'm not sure this is for you, but ..."
- "How would you feel if this time next year ..."
- "Just imagine ..."
- "If you're like me ..."
- "What most people do is ..."
- "The good news is ..."

◆ *Prepare for setbacks* – Change rarely happens the way we plan it. Another way we could define resilience is: how we respond when things don't go as planned. When beginning a change or initiative, understand that there will be setbacks, hiccups, and unforeseen problems. This is normal and to be expected.

◆ *Avoid, "yeah, but"* – When facing change (and the challenges that come along with it), there may be times when the response or thinking becomes defensive. This is natural; it's protective and survival oriented in nature. When you find yourself in that defensive and excuse-focused mindset, challenge yourself to think differently. Say things to yourself like, "I've seen this before. I know what to do" and "I've tackled difficult things before. I can do this too." In addition, remind yourself what educator and innovation expert George Couros says, "Change is an opportunity to do something amazing" (2020).

◆ *Understand the emotions* – Change, particularly change that is forced upon us, often brings with it feelings of frustration and anxiety. Negative emotions – ones we experience and express as well as ones expressed by our staff – are normal and to be expected.

◆ *Focus on control* – You've heard this theme several times throughout the book – manage stress by focusing on what you can control. In fact, Robert Sapolsky, in the groundbreaking book *Why Zebras Don't Get Ulcers* (2004) says to focus on "footholds of control" – areas where you have control, influence, and are able to see progress. When feeling the stress that comes with change, repeat this to yourself, "I cannot control everything and I should not control everything."

◆ *Teach staff about change* – When implementing change (a new curricular program, for example) teach staff not only about the why (the rationale for the change) and the what (the new program) but teach them about the process of change. Help them to understand the role of emotions, what happens when things don't go as planned, how to collaborate around successes and challenges, and how to seek help.

◆ *Then remember, change is really hard* – Changing human behavior is difficult. Once habits are in place, they are very hard to change. But as leaders if we focus on initiating the right kinds of behavior from the *beginning*, we are better off. Changing bad habits takes a lot of effort. But when we put our efforts into creating the right kind of habits and thinking patterns from the start, it is easier to manage and deal with change.

◆ *Allow staff to fail* – Implementing new things can get messy. When things become messy, staff may experience fear. Specifically, a fear of failure. The fear of failure can be a significant barrier to change. In fact, "driving out fear" is one of the actions that build a capacity for change, according to Reginald Green (2009) in *Practicing the Art of Leadership*.

14

Resilient School Leaders – Become Experts in Conflict

In a Nutshell ✅

Conflict, whether we like it or not, is a daily part of school leadership. Effective school leaders not only understand the nature of conflict (and the stressors that accompany it), they utilize specific tools and methods to guide themselves and their staff through conflict.

Digging Deeper 🔍

First off, we might be stretching it a bit to state that a resilient school leader needs to become "an expert" in conflict. Expertise requires a depth of knowledge and experience that not everyone possess equally. But, at the very least, school leaders need to have an understanding of how conflict manifests itself in the organization and a knowledge of effective tools to address it.

The influential American educator and scholar John Dewey famously stated that conflict is "the gadfly of thought." We don't use the term "gadfly" much anymore; a gadfly is simply

DOI: 10.4324/9781003301356-14

an annoyance. It is something or someone that pesters, irritates, criticizes, and prompts us to take action. He had a point. Conflict can stir us to action and cause us to focus on something that needs to change. Dewey goes on to say that conflict can actually result in positive change and ingenuity.

Working off Dewey's premise (that good things can arise from conflict), we'll take it another step. Conflict is necessary, vital, and empowering. We know, that's a strong claim. Let us prove it to you.

First, a few definitions and baselines to ground the discussion:

♦ The way we'll define conflict is a bit simplistic but it works – conflict is simply when someone or something is in the way. You have a goal, an expectation, a belief, or a desire to act, and something or someone is preventing (or partially preventing) you from getting what you want. That's conflict. Conflict is not always the result of goal-oriented behavior, of course. Sometimes conflict comes from miscommunication, misunderstandings, or competing values. But in its essence, conflict is about the barriers and obstacles that are in our way.

♦ Conflict, the way we typically think about it, is a negative thing. When you consider synonyms of the concept – *strong disagreement, power struggles, opposition, friction, discord, etc.* – they all evoke a negative feeling or connotation. It's no wonder many of us try to avoid conflict.

♦ Our society is fragmented and fractured over just about everything. From politics to climate to religion to sports – you name it. People disagree and they disagree strongly at times. Blame it on social media, the mass media, politicians, or on the general state of human nature – it's often very hard to find agreement on things. When there is strong disagreement there is conflict.

♦ There aren't a lot of effective conflict resolution models in our society. Actually, that's not quite true. There *are* models and examples of effective conflict resolution out there; they just don't get much attention. Consider what gets the most attention in the news and on social media – the loud, the profane, the extreme. It's no wonder that our students, our families, and some of our staff don't have productive conflict resolution skills.

◆ Conflict is simply a byproduct of being around people. If we lead people, we need to expect that we'll be in conflict. It just *is*. If conflict is a natural part of being around people, we need to expect it. Resilient school leaders are not surprised, frustrated, or depressed about conflict. We don't necessarily go looking for conflict, but we are not surprised when it happens.

◆ Not only is conflict unavoidable (because we spend our day around people), it can actually be a really good thing. Clarification – the *right* kind of conflict can be a really good thing. Keep reading, we'll discuss the difference between good conflict and not-so-good conflict.

◆ Conflict is stressful. Enough said!

The right kind of conflict is a wonderful thing that can spur growth, plant seeds for improvement, and actually improve relationships. So, what is the difference between good conflict that helps us to improve and bad conflict that keeps us stuck?

Allen Amason (2007), a management researcher from Georgia Southern University, describes two kinds of conflict: *cognitive* and *affective*. Affective conflict focuses on feelings, past experiences, emotions, and typically centers on people or events. Cognitive conflict, on the other hand, focuses on ideas, issues, or processes. While both exist and are often intertwined, cognitive conflict – where the disagreement focuses on ideas and outcomes rather than personalities and past events – is productive and necessary for a healthy organization. Here is a simplistic, but accurate, way to think about – we want cognitive conflict; we don't want affective conflict.

Think of cognitive conflict as centering on ideas. As an example, let's say that you want to initiate a program at your school that is focused on improving communication with families. You call together a committee to brainstorm strategies. When the focus of the conversation is on the ideas – even when there is strong disagreement – that's a healthy thing. We want to be surrounded by people who can challenge us to think differently, to consider alternative perspectives, or to try new and different ideas. The key is that the conflict (the disagreement) is focused on the ideas, not the people. If the focus is on the ideas, you'll likely be productive. However, if the disagreement centers on the people (especially when you are working with people that you don't particularly like all that much), you'll be stuck.

Application Points

- ◆ *What kind?* – The next time you find yourself in a conflict, ask yourself, "Is this affective or cognitive?" Identifying the type of conflict you are experiencing is necessary in order to consider how to address it. Is the focus of the conflict on people and past offenses or is it on the ideas and strategies? The more we can focus our efforts on the ideas, the better off everyone will be.
- ◆ *Am I mixing the two?* – Here is a sad truth – when we dislike someone (or a group of someones) because of past affective conflicts, we tend to disregard *all* their ideas, even the good ones. It's a challenge to listen to people that we don't particularly like. But effective leadership requires that we listen to everyone. Part of effective listening is understanding that good ideas can (and often do) come from sources that we don't particularly like all that much.
- ◆ *Speaking of listening* – Now may be a good time to go back to Chapter 11 and review some of what we discussed regarding the brain's two thinking systems – fast and slow. You'll see how the ideas are relevant and applicable to our discussion of conflict.
- ◆ *Separate person from idea* – When people disagree, they often attack the other person's character, intelligence, or motivations. While this is common, it's not healthy or productive. When working through a conflict, do your

best to make a distinction between the person and their ideas. This is not always easy, of course. People tend to identify themselves with their ideas. We all do that. Part of our identity is attached to what we believe but it's good to remember that we can all be wrong at times.

◆ *Remove pronouns* – Use language that depersonalizes the conflict. As much as possible, remove terms like *I, they, us, we,* and *them.* While others may use lots of pronouns in describing the problem, we do everyone a great service when we focus on the issue(s) rather than the people. Use phrases like, "The main issue to be addressed is …" rather than "You seem to think that there is a problem with the way we …" This process, by the way, will help to *separate person from idea.*

◆ *Challenge the win–lose mentality* – When we are in conflict with someone, particularly one who is a rival or adversary, the shift in focus often veers towards win–lose. When we are in such a state, listening and understanding take a back seat to winning. Here is a good reflection question – "Do I want to *be* right or do I want to *make* it right?"

◆ *Don't rehearse too much* – When anticipating conflict, here is what most of us do: we rehearse. We role play in our minds what we *think* will happen during the conflict. We try to predict what the other person/party will say and what we'll say in response. The problem is that the actual interaction rarely plays out how we rehearsed in our minds. That's a lot of wasted worry and stress.

◆ *Don't be surprised* – Resilient leaders don't necessarily wake up each morning wishing for conflict, but they're not surprised by it either. Remember that conflict simply *is*; it's a natural outcome of spending time with people. And understand that many of our students, families, and staff have not developed effective conflict management techniques. So, we are not only unsurprised by the existence of conflict in the organization, we are also not surprised that some people will possess less-than-productive ways to deal with it.

◆ *Quit taking it personally (QTIP)* – It's not always easy to do but is important to understand that much of the time the behavior of other people says more about them (their past experiences, their assumptions, their beliefs) than it does about you. While you may be the current target, you may not be the *cause* of the conflict. If or when we take things too personally, we could become too involved to understand different perspectives accurately.

◆ *Understand confirmation bias* – Confirmation bias is the tendency to find and interpret information to confirm what you already know or believe about something. We all experience this on a daily basis; we find and prioritize evidence that supports what we believe. When we are in conflict, we need to be aware that our bias will be towards what we already believe the outcomes should be, and we'll hold on intently to evidence that supports our assumptions. And, perhaps more importantly, we'll tend to disregard information that demonstrates that we may be wrong about something. When we are in conflict, particularly affective conflict, we want to be right and that desire will lead us to finding and holding on only to evidence or information that supports our assumptions and beliefs.

◆ *Understand that conflict may cue ANTs* – Conflict, even cognitive conflict, often brings with it strong emotions. Those strong emotions can trigger us to negative thinking. We'll dive more into these ideas in Chapter 19 but simply be aware that when you are in conflict, less-than-productive thinking patterns may appear including ANTs – automatic negative thoughts.

◆ *Practice reframing* – We reference this strategy a lot, but for good reason. When we can reframe a situation or adjust our thinking about a problem we are facing, it opens us up to new ways of solving the problem. Instead of saying something like, "This is a staff member who just not open to new ideas" say, "This is a staff member who wants to make sure that their efforts will show positive outcomes for kids before they try something new."

◆ *Give up the need to be right* – Or, more specifically, give up the need to *always* be right. Let's admit it, as leaders, some of us are control freaks. Part of being a control freak is the need to be right (or to have others believe we are right). This can be a recipe of disaster. This means that we sometimes need to "lose the battle to win the war."

◆ *Go looking for conflict* – OK, we admit – this sounds strange. But consider this: if you are not challenging yourself to learn, grow, and try new things, you are being hypocritical. Every day we ask our students and our staff to learn and grow. Part of learning and growth is challenging ideas and thoughts. When we are challenged, we'll feel conflict.

15

Resilient School Leaders – Know How to Deal with Difficult People

In a Nutshell

Difficult people cannot be avoided. We don't really need to say much more. Well, maybe we'll say this – you are not likely going to have much success trying to change a difficult person into a cooperative one. While you cannot change them, you can adjust the way you respond to them.

Digging Deeper

It may help if we start with a basic question – *why are difficult people so difficult?* Why are they the way they are? What is the payoff for their behavior? What makes them tick? And, most importantly, how should we respond when working with a difficult person?

Actually, before we dig into those questions, let's define it – what *is* a difficult person? This is a bit more challenging than it may seem because the term "difficult" is rather abstract. *Difficult* will mean different things to different people. Is a person difficult

DOI: 10.4324/9781003301356-15

because they complain a lot? Or is it someone who whines, or brags, or who consistently violates rules, or one who tries to do the minimum amount of work possible to stay out of trouble? Maybe the difficult person can be characterized as a narcissist who makes everything about themselves. Or maybe it's a person who is aggressive or mean. A difficult person might even be an agreeable one who gives lip service but never follows through on commitments.

You may be thinking, "Yes! It's all of those plus a lot more."

For our simple purposes here, let's use a common dictionary definition – "someone who is difficult behaves in an unreasonable and unhelpful way" (dictionary.reverso.net). Quite simply, a difficult person makes it hard to do our jobs. They exhibit certain traits (lack of compassion, little concern for the opinions of others, callousness, bullying, etc.) that are antagonistic to the functioning of healthy organizations.

Now, let's address the question, *why are these people so difficult?*

To get to an answer, we can use a process that most school leaders are familiar with – a functional behavioral assessment (FBA). Most of us are accustomed to conducting some sort of FBA when working with students, perhaps as part of the special education Individualized Education Plan (IEP) process. The FBA process works quite well for this discussion also. In essence, an FBA attempts to answer the question, "Why is the behavior happening?" before attempting to utilize specific methods or strategies.

The same process can be used to help us understand the behavior of the adults around us. Namely, we spend time thinking about the *function* of the behavior. The function is the payoff. All behavior has a payoff; even when the result or consequence of the behavior is a negative one. An easy way to think about this is by using the acronym EATS as in "Everyone EATS." All behavior serves a function or underlying reason that can generally be put into a few categories represented by EATS – is the behavior an attempt to *escape* something? Is the behavior an attempt at *attention*? Is the behavior an attempt at getting something *tangible* or there a need for something *sensory*? This is a simplistic way to view behavior, of course. Behavior is always complex and multicausal. And, people, even mature adults, don't always really know what is driving their behaviors or tendencies. But we do ourselves and our staff a service by starting with the question, what is the payoff for their behavior? That's our starting point when working with difficult people – attempting to understand what drives their behavior.

Even when we do our best to understand why (and we maintain our composure around challenging people) there will be times when, as a leader, you'll need to confront a person about their behavior. Let's dig into some tools and tips for those difficult times when confrontation is necessary.

◆ Prepare ahead of time – plan out some talking points and major topics to discuss. Keep it brief – address one topic or behavior at a time. Do your best to avoid bringing up past events or past conflicts. Doing so will likely put that person on the defensive.

◆ When the need arises to confront a negative person, do so privately in order to help them maintain their dignity. If needed, based on bad prior experiences, bring along a witness or third party that both of you trust.

◆ During the meeting, be as descriptive as possible about the challenging behavior without using judgmental phrases. One easy way to do that is by removing pronouns. Instead of saying something like, "I felt frustrated when you made such negative comments during the staff meeting. Everyone was shocked that you would talk to me in that manner" say "The issue regarding the comments made during the staff meeting needs to be addressed."

◆ Remember that it is an act of love and respect to address unhealthy behavior. When bad behavior is allowed to persist, it may become a habit and will likely have a negative impact on the school culture.

You might be interested to learn that some excellent academic research has addressed questions related to difficult people. We'll point you to the work of Dr. Chelsea Sleep from the University of Georgia. She and her colleagues have developed the Difficult

Person Test (www.idrlabs.com/difficult-person/test.php) that provides data and feedback on personality characteristics such as aggressiveness, grandiosity, and suspiciousness. Although we would not suggest that you ask your staff to complete the survey as part of a staff meeting; that might be sending the wrong message.

Application Points

◆ *Remember conflict* – Now might be a good time to review some of what was discussed in Chapter 14 Resilient School Leaders Become Experts in Conflict. Namely, when working with challenging people, consider they type of conflict you are experiencing (affective or cognitive).

◆ *Remember that we are all creatures of habit* – Much of our behavior is habitual rather than thoughtful. When counseling, guiding, or leading a challenging person, ask questions to get them to reflect on their behavior.

◆ *Quit taking it personally (QTIP)* – This application point was offered in the previous chapter as well. And, in full disclosure, it is going to show up again in one of the upcoming chapters. That's because it is a powerfully effective tool. Taking things too personally only pulls you into unnecessary conflict. The truth is that most of the challenging behavior you have to deal with in others has very little to with you.

◆ *Unless it does* – We just suggested that you QTIP – avoid taking things too personally. And, as you know, most peoples' behavior really has little to do with you. It really has to do with their own background experiences, personality, and coping mechanisms. But, there's a catch – sometimes it does. Sometimes the challenging behaviors we are dealing with in others *is* a result of something we've done. Effective leaders walk a fine line between QTIP and personal reflection and humility. Reflect on questions such as, "Are my behaviors or responses making things worse?" or "Did any of my behaviors start or worsen this conflict?"

◆ *Accept them for who they are* – You've no doubt heard the mantra "You can't change people." While we mostly agree with this (because people have to change themselves), you can influence, teach, and guide them to reflect on their behaviors, habits, and tendencies. And remember that difficult people have strengths (sometimes significant ones) that you, as a leader, need to tap into.

◆ *Adopt the mindset, "different, not difficult"* – Much of building your personal resilience is reminding yourself to think differently about the challenges in front of you. Whether you refer to it as self-talk or inner dialogue, the idea is that we can gain control (and manage our stress better) by simply choosing to reframe a situation. That "difficult" person may simply be one who thinks or acts very differently from you.

◆ *Realize that* ***you*** *are someone's difficult person* – As odd a thought as it may seem, every single one of us is someone else's difficult person. Here is a bit of a reality check – there is someone (maybe many someones) who look at you and see a difficult, challenging, or hard-to-handle personality. As good as you are in most areas of your life – as much as you are loved and admired by most people around you – there is someone who, when they think of you, go "Ugh. I can't stand that person." That's humbling. When someone views us as challenging, we wish to have them deal with us in a patient, understanding, and positive manner. We owe the same thing to others.

◆ *Respond rather than react* – Good leaders take the time to consider how they'll respond to difficult and challenging situations. While we are all guilty of reacting in ineffective ways, the best leaders are ones who give thoughtful and productive responses. In addition, under times of extreme conflict, you may need to put yourself in check by doing the opposite of your first reaction. Take time to reflect, think, and plan prior to interacting with a negative person in a challenging situation. Avoid being pulled into battles, particularly emotional ones. Negative people often thrive on the conflict. Or, they may not have effective coping mechanisms when things get tense.

◆ *"No" doesn't always mean "no"* – Remember that an initial reluctance or resistance on someone's part does not mean that they will forever be a "no" on a particular idea or concept. Some people just need more time. Some are slow adopters who need evidence and proof before they'll expend effort. And some people just need complain a bit before they jump into wholesale change.

◆ *Limit your time* – If you let them, negative people will suck the joy right out of you. In fact, there is evidence that spending too much time around negative people will increase your own sense of cynicism and burnout (Skovholt & Trotter-Mathison, 2016). While we cannot always avoid negative people, we can control how we interact with them and how much of our time they get.

◆ *Presume positive intentions* – Dr. Robert Garmston, the highly influential American educator and expert in cognitive coaching and group facilitation, reminds us to presume/assume that the motives, thinking, and intentions of others is coming from a positive place. While the behaviors they demonstrate might not be positive, we work from a better position when we assume that the motivations of the other party are positive.

16

Resilient School Leaders – Take Risks

In a Nutshell ✓

When we take risks, we'll fail (assuming we take risks that push us enough). Resilient leaders know how to respond emotionally and cognitively. How we respond is what makes us resilient or not. After all, rebounding from a setback is the definition of resilience.

Digging Deeper

Regardless of where you are in your career, you should be pushing yourself to learn, grow, and try new things. You should be challenging old habits, cleaning out the toolbox of leadership practices that may not be effective, and working hard to refine your abilities to lead. After all, isn't constant improvement and growth what you are asking of your students and staff?

Keep in mind that taking risks often coincides with failure. Mistakes are made, things don't go as planned, doubt and worry may set in. McGregor and Elliot (2005) explain that when a change

DOI: 10.4324/9781003301356-16

or challenge is unfamiliar, it may cause us to sense a loss of control. When control is lost, emotions may be taxed and shame or fear may set in. Or, individuals may experience a sense of hopelessness when a setback happens (Thrall, McNicol, & McElrath, 1999). The good news is that it's OK to fail. We just need to learn how to fail forward.

Resilient leaders plan for failure. Note that we didn't say that resilient leaders plan *to* fail. When pushing forward and trying new things, failure will most likely happen, but it's OK, failure doesn't define a resilient person (Reivich & Shatte, 2002). Instead, the lessons learned will be applied to the future with a goal of improvement. Maxwell Maltz's famous quote is a good reminder, "You make mistakes. Mistakes don't make you."

Mistakes that are acknowledged and dealt with demonstrate a level of humility and openness. These traits will actually lead to increased credibility in the eyes of those you lead. Credibility is the foundation of leadership. Consider what leadership gurus Kouzes and Posner (1987) said, "Managers get other people to do, but leaders get other people to want to do. Leaders do this by first of all being credible." This is our essential idea – when mistakes are made, effective leaders recognize them, own up to them, and do what is in their power to make things right. When we try to cover things up, even when we try to downplay the effects of our mistakes on others, it can lead to significant levels of distrust among our staff.

It's also important to note that failure can be a good thing. When we fail, we can use it as a teachable moment where we process what happened and learn from it. It may be emotional or frustrating, but how we respond is what makes us resilient or not. Think about all the times you asked your students and staff to stretch themselves and to "step outside of their comfort zone" to try new things. Essentially, we ask them to set aside their fears and try something new. Are we, as leaders, also taking risks and stepping outside of our comfort zones?

Part of the challenge, of course, is that taking risks (for leaders) is a public endeavor. If we succeed, great. Everyone sees it. If we fail, everyone sees that also. This helps to explain why so many of us struggle to try new things; it's a fear of failure (and, to no small extent, a fear of failing in a public way where everyone takes notice).

As you strive to improve (which requires some risk-taking), consider the importance of setting goals. In the classic book *See You at the Top* (1975), author Zig Ziglar explains that you can't hit a target that you don't have. If you want specific success, you have to have a specific goal. Once the goal is in motion, Ziglar reminds us that, "when obstacles arise, you change your direction to reach your goal; you do not change your decision to get there." Similarly, author Shawn Achor in *The Happiness Advantage* (2018) describes what he refers to as The Zorro Effect where we gain big victories by first focusing first on smaller ones. He reminds us that we are better off when we create smaller goals (ones that still stretch us a bit) and experience success on those. Success leads to success. If you want to write a book, you start by writing one page. If you want to get in shape or learn a new skill, take it one day at a time.

Resiliency is how we think and what we do after facing an adverse situation. Sometimes we just have to be motivated by what we know and not by what we see. We know that taking risks with the possibility of failure can build resilience, even if don't see immediate results. We know that having a growth mindset where we thrive on new challenges helps us to use failure as a way to improve our abilities.

As we try new things and take risks, remember that growth is rarely linear. There will be setbacks. Keep moving forward, take risks, find joy in the process, and believe that the outcome (even if it's only building more resiliency and figuring out what *not* to do) will be beneficial in the end.

Application Points

- *Stop comparing yourself to others* – Often our reluctance to take risks stems from a habit of comparing ourselves to others or worrying too much about what others might think (especially if we fail to meet our goals). You've likely heard this before, but it is worth repeating – "Comparison is the thief of joy" – attributed to Theodore Roosevelt. If we go a bit deeper, consider this: when we compare ourselves to others, the result is either pride or envy. Pride if ware better than someone else, envy if we are not. Those are not good internal states for leaders. Nor are they good for stress management.

◆ *Remember, you will probably fail* – If you create a goal that sufficiently stretches you, there is a good chance you'll not meet that goal. But that's OK. If you always meet your goals, you are likely not pushing yourself enough.

◆ *Find the meaning* – Resilient people derive meaning from failure (Reivich and Shatte, 2002). That is, failure does not define the resilient person. They use lessons learned to improve in the future.

◆ *Write it down* – List your goals, dreams, and aspirations. There is power in externalizing your vision and dreams for your organization. That vision likely includes some element of change. As you work to formalize your goals and ideas for change, write them down, edit them over time, and ask for feedback from a trusted colleague.

◆ *Plan ahead* – Anticipate ahead of time how you might respond if you fail or hit a roadblock. Think about what options, actions, and personal supports will help you recover from those setbacks.

◆ *Allow the emotion* – If you try something new and fail to meet your own expectations, you'll likely experience feelings of frustration, annoyance, or even some anger. As Bryan highlighted in *17 Things Resilient Teachers Do* (2021), resilient people don't try to control their emotions. Emotions cannot be controlled. But they can be managed. The first step to managing emotions is to recognize and allow the emotion (albeit for a short period of time). Allow the emotion and then ask, "What do I need to do in order to manage myself into a better emotion?"

◆ *Learn new stuff* – If you don't consistently challenge yourself to learn new content, skills, and ideas, you're a hypocrite. That is what you ask of your students and staff everyday – try something new, take a risk, learn something, step outside your comfort zone. And, going one level deeper, it is often those staff that are "stuck in their ways" that frustrate us the most. In what ways might you be stuck in your ways?

◆ *Reflect on the hurts, mistakes, and failures ... then let go* – Using what you gained from the failure, consider a broader range of possibilities and opportunities when approaching a similar situation in the future. Use these sentence stems to practice:

- I elect to leave _____ in the past. I will do this by focusing on ...
- I choose to emphasize _____ in the future. I will do this by focusing on ...

◆ *Push yourself* – The book *The Science of Mastering Life's Greatest Challenges* (2018) tells us to do things that scare us. There is good evidence that suggests we can relax the fear networks in the brain by consistently challenging ourselves to try new things. We can actually become less fearful with practice.

◆ *Remember, you are modeling* – Thrall et al.'s 1999 book, The *Ascent of a Leader*, said it perfectly, "To take risks, we need to feel a certain degree of safety and security in our environment. We lose hope when we sense no room for the occasional misstep or setback. Without hope, we cease to dream about possibilities." Our staff and students need to see us taking risks. They need to know that they'll also need to take risks but they'll do so in an environment of grace, patience, and understanding.

◆ *Set goals* – OK, this one seems too obvious, so why did we restate it? Our point is that it's not just about setting goals, it's about setting the *right* goals. In the 2017 book *The Leading Brain: Powerful Science-Based Strategies for Achieving Peak Performance*, authors Fabritius and Hageman say, "If the goal you set doesn't make your eyes light up when you think of it. Or if you feel no fear in the possibility of failing to reach it, then it probably isn't a good goal for you."

◆ *Seek the OS!M* – One of the best leadership books you may never have heard of is *The Radical Leap* (2004) by Steve Farber. In it he says, "The ability to lead doesn't come from a snappy vocabulary, the books you've displayed on your shelves, your place on the organizational chart, or that fashionable title on your business card. Leadership is always substantive and rarely fashionable. It is intensely personal and intrinsically scary, and it requires us to live the ideas we espouse – in irrefutable ways – every day of our lives, up to and beyond the point of fear." Fear, as you've seen, is a central theme to taking risks and trying new things. Farber tells leaders to seek OS!Ms – "Oh Sh&^! Moments" – when we attempt to do something that truly frightens us or scares us out of our minds (because of the fear of failure), that's an OS!M. Farber goes on to highlight that we've been conditioned to think that fear is a bad thing. But fear is a natural part of growth. In fact, true personal growth rarely happens without some level of fear.

17

Resilient School Leaders – Help Others Build Resilience

In a Nutshell ✓

Helping others in their understanding of the role of stress and resiliency (and helping to equip them with effective tools and strategies) is a gift that will last a lifetime. Plus, that gift can help to accomplish important school-wide goals such as academic growth, improved student behavior, and positive staff morale.

Digging Deeper 🔍

Now is a good time for a quick review of some of our most important understandings about stress and resilience. Before we attempt to assist, lead, or train others, there are a few things that we need to make sure are solid in our understanding and personal practice. Some key ideas include:

♦ Stress is all about control. More specifically, stress is a result of a perception of a lack of control. When we believe that we have little to no control over something,

DOI: 10.4324/9781003301356-17

it stresses us out. We don't get stressed about things that are within our control, only those things that are not.

◆ Stress is a good thing. Humans hit peak performance when there is the right balance of stress, pressure, realistic goals, and support. Too much or too little stress results in poorer performance. To learn more about this balance, do a web search for the *Yerkes-Dodson Model*.

◆ The healthy kind of stress is called *eustress*. This happens when we experience a short dose of discomfort or anxiety followed by a quick recovery time. Think about a rollercoaster ride, a first date, a job interview, or having a baby (although some parents might say, "It's been a few years and we're still not recovered!"). The fact is that you want stress in your life; or more accurately, you want manageable stress in your life.

◆ Stress is contagious. In a widely cited 2016 study, researchers found a direct link between student stress levels and teacher stress levels (Oberle & Schonert-Reichl, 2016). While that study found a link between teachers and students, we also understand that as leaders we have tremendous influence over student and staff stress levels. Interestingly, the opposite may be true as well. In the book *Connected: The Surprising Power of Our Social Networks and How They Shape Our Lives* (2011), authors James Fowler and Nicholas Christakas point out that positivity is "socially contagious."

Using a tool such as the Search Institute's Developmental Assets Survey, have your staff and students consider their own strengths using some sort of assessment or survey. For example, a question in the Development Assets Survey asks individuals to consider both internal and external assets. Why is this important? Resilience and growth are built from a person's strengths, not their weaknesses. Herein lies one of our most significant challenges – as educators we are well trained at identifying, diagnosing, and attending to *weaknesses*. This makes sense, of course, when considering academics. As educators, it is our job to figure out what individual children need and then devise a plan to meet those needs. For example, if a child enters 3rd grade below standards in reading comprehension, we do our best to diagnose the problem and then create a plan to address the problem so that the child catches up and ultimately excels. Essentially, we are aiming to fill the gap.

This way of thinking – identifying and addressing academic weaknesses or gaps – is appropriate and necessary in the academic realm, but it does not work when trying to help someone develop resilience (or any positive behavior, for that matter). For someone to develop a personal skill like resilience, we always work from a position of strength. Strengths and assets are the foundation; the foundation or starting point cannot be a weakness. This, by the way, is one of the reasons we are so adamant that reframing (cognitive reappraisal) is necessary. Speaking of reframing, we saw this recently on the web and thought it fit perfectly in this discussion: *when you are tempted to label a child "attention-seeking" refer to them as "connection-seeking" instead.* The way we label and think about people matters. A lot.

An important note – throughout the book you may have gotten the impression that resiliency is one thing. In fact, it's not. Seminal resilience researchers Steven and Sybil Wolin (1996) found that over time, it was possible to rise above adversities by developing certain skills. They identified seven specific types of resilience. Additionally, while we're mentioning it, now is a good time to acknowledge some of the other seminal work that has been done on the topic of resilience. For example, Henderson and Milstein (2003) offer many resources for building resiliency and inner strength with students and staff in a school setting. They particularly focus on moving students from at-risk to resilient. Insider tip – try referring to students (at least in your own thinking) as "at hope" not "at risk."

Other resiliency researchers, such as Werner and Smith (1992), studied how high-risk children overcome the odds. They followed over 500 individuals for 30+ years to understand how stressful life events and childhood adversity impacted their lives over time. Many overcame the troubles to have a healthy, well-rounded life. One additional researcher that is important to note is Bonnie Benard. She has decades of research that focus particularly on the role that families, schools, and community play in resilient children. Specifically, she addresses how resiliency prevails even in extreme cases where children are impacted by poverty, neighborhood violence, and a dysfunctional home life.

Why does this matter? While it may seem that the topic of resilience is new (particularly with the use of a term like "grit"), there is actually a deep well of research that informs our thinking. Resilience and the ability to manage stressors, some would argue, is a bit like helping someone build character. Traditionally, those tasks (building character, helping someone work through adversity, etc.) were the responsibility of the family. Many (maybe most) families still adopt this responsibility, of course. But unfortunately, in this fast-paced world we live in, it seems that many families have either forgotten or surrendered that responsibility. So, we could hope for the best with our students and staff, or we could help them learn how to become more resilient.

Combined we've (Janet and Bryan) spent over 50 years teaching and leading in school and district settings. From Kindergarten to higher education, we've done it all (almost) in the profession. We love the profession. We love students and teachers and families and the greater education community. We're lifers. And we believe there is far more right, good, and effective in our schools than society or the media would like to acknowledge.

With that said, can we do some honest reflection for a moment? An honest reflection about the state of many of our schools. Schools are not always great at building resiliency and stress management in students or staff. Many schools are high stress environments because of things like large class sizes, too few opportunities for personal or creative pursuits, a hyper focus on academic achievement often at the expense of everything else, high staff turnover, lack of financial resources, being understaffed, etc. That list could go on and on. Almost all of us could recount stories of great educators and leaders who left the profession, never to return. The stress was just too much. Too much stress, too little pay. Too much stress, too little support. After all, it's tough to work so hard and see so few results.

But, there is hope! There is evidence indicating that teachers with higher levels of resilience stay in the profession longer (Mullen, Shields, & Tienken, 2021). This is true of leaders and administrators, as well, of course. And, as you'll learn when you do your own deeper dive into some of the researchers we mentioned previously, you'll find that students do better in school (and life) when they have higher levels of resilience. We're willing to be that you are already convinced of these facts, or you wouldn't have made it to Chapter 17 of the book!

Application Points

♦ *Teach about stress and resilience* – If the ideas and concepts shared throughout this book have been helpful, share them with students, staff, and parents. You don't need to become an expert to start sharing tidbits, examples of research, anecdotes, and strategies. Start small, but start. As an example, there is good evidence that when students are taught how to view stressful events in a positive manner, they experience better outcomes and are more open to receiving feedback (Crum, Salovey, & Achor, 2013). Additionally, realize that the word "stress" has been abused in our culture. Stress is not a bad thing. Stress is good. Your brain/body was designed to experience stress. Don't carelessly throw around "stress" assuming it is always a bad thing.

♦ *Words matter* – Stop telling kids, staff, parents (or anyone else for that matter) that they have anxiety. Instead teach them specific methods to practice resiliency when they start to feel anxious. For example, teach them about the power of self-talk and help them to identify *automatic negative thoughts* (more about ANTs in Chapter 19).

♦ *Make an affirmation* – Teach people how to affirm the best of who they are. Affirmations build resiliency by overcoming negative thoughts and affirming positive characteristics. "I am" statements can be powerful in shaping thoughts and behaviors.

◆ *Shift the focus* – When leading teachers and staff (particularly during times of challenge and change), shift the conversations from "What do I teach?" and "How do I teach it?" to "What is my impact?" Then, ask questions focused on what approaches are most likely to get the intended impact?

◆ *Get writing* – Handwritten notes of encouragement are powerful things. Note and elaborate on what you see as strengths in your teachers, students, parents, and staff.

◆ *Make time to teach* – Be intentional and make resiliency and stress management a topic of preservice meetings and monthly staff meetings.

◆ *Change your role* – Go into the classroom and take over lessons for teachers. Then have the teacher evaluate you and provide feedback. This can reduce stress (and build respect and understanding) if teachers can give you feedback about what they view as your instructional strengths. Think about how powerful this will be when you, as the leader, have to do the teachers' annual evaluation.

◆ *Model, model, model* – Model the very behaviors you expect to see in your staff. This is particularly important for those on your staff that may want to enter formal leadership positions. As leaders, if we give lip service to, for example, the importance of going home at a reasonable hour but our future prospective leaders see us working until 7 or 8 at night, they'll believe what they see, not what you tell them.

◆ *Create "I'm Great" files* – An "I'm Great" file is a reminder of your impact. We offered this suggestion in Chapter 4 as well. Help students and staff create their own "I'm Great" files.

◆ *Tell stories* – Stories are powerful things. Stories spark interest, engage thinking, and connect to emotions. Yes, they tend to be anecdotal, and some staff might dismiss them as inconsequential, but stories can help open up possibilities and opportunities to reflect on stress management and resilience.

◆ *Teach the difference between assertive and aggressive* – Being assertive means that you advocate or your interests (or the interests of others). You can be assertive and still be kind, respectful, and genuine. Being aggressive means that you attack the interests of the other person. When being aggressive, we usually resort to less than respectful behaviors to get our point across.

◆ *Analyze your systems* – One study (Skaalvik, & Skaalvik, 2021) indicated that most of the work-related stressors that staff experience come in the form of organizational demands and the methods of communication from administrators. Take time to analyze and get feedback about the systems in your school. Ask, "Is there a responsibility, task, or duty placed upon my staff that is unnecessary?" Now might also be a good time to address a common (but incomplete) argument – if teachers just took better care of themselves, things would improve. While we partially agree with this idea – it does not excuse the systematic challenges that they face. Budget shortfalls, unrealistic political pressures, societal and family issues – those all exacerbate the problem. Just telling educators to take better care of themselves won't address such issues.

◆ *Take 3 minutes* – Our friend and colleague, LaVonna Roth (www.igniteyourshine.com) suggests that each and every staff member do this reflective exercise regularly during the school year: take 3 minutes and write down everything you did that day related to your job. Then put a star next to those things that are mandatory. Then take a look at those things that do not have stars and ask, can any of these things be removed? Part of this activity also includes placing a "heart" next to those things that may not be mandatory but are things that the staff member loves; those things that give them joy and energy. This activity helps to analyze what is "on your plate" that is necessary and what is not. Specifically, it forces us to consider what can be removed that may not be necessary. It also helps us to identify those things that we enjoy about our jobs.

18

Resilient School Leaders – Forgive and Apologize

In a Nutshell ✓

Forgiveness is an intentional process where we make a decision to release feelings of anger or resentment. It is a way to move forward, beyond the emotions, for your own sake and for the sake of others. Whether others deserve it or not, forgiveness provides a concrete and powerful method to manage stress and build resilience.

Digging Deeper

To frame our discussion, let's consider what others have stated about the power of forgiveness:

- ◆ "Sometimes we forgive not because we are wrong but because staying angry robs us of happiness." – Anonymous
- ◆ "It's not an easy journey, to get to a place where you forgive people. But it is such a powerful place, because it frees you." – Tyler Perry

DOI: 10.4324/9781003301356-18

- ◆ "Sometimes people haven't apologized because they're ashamed. Forgive them anyway. Sometimes you have to be OK with the sorry you never got." – Anonymous
- ◆ "Forgiveness is valued by all societies and faiths. But many people struggle to forgive." – John Templeton Foundation
- ◆ "The weak can never forgive. Forgiveness is the attribute of the strong." – Mahatma Gandhi
- ◆ "When I was a kid, I used to pray every night for a new bicycle. Then I realized that the Lord doesn't work that way so I stole one and asked Him to forgive me." – Emo Philips

OK, that last quote from comedian Emo Phillips is a bit of a stretch. We included it to see if you were paying attention and to provide a bit of levity to a serious topic.

Part of being a school leader is understanding that people will talk about you (yes, they gossip, a lot), they'll criticize you unfairly, they'll hold grudges, and they'll seek revenge for perceived slights. We make being a school leader sound like a lot of fun, don't we? While criticism comes with the job title, the act of forgiving and apologizing is a learned skill; a powerful and effective one that will help you tap into wells of strength and resilience that you may not be aware of.

Let's start by defining what it is. Forgiveness is a deliberate attempt to cope with or overcome an unhappy feeling after experiencing a situation of mistreatment (Pargament, 1997). The key idea here is that forgiveness (and all the messy emotions that accompany mistreatment) is a deliberate act. It requires a change in perception and belief, primarily on the part of the person providing the forgiveness. It is the act of extending grace to others. Grace, by definition, is providing some benefit where it is not deserved. Others may not "deserve" our forgiveness; grace gives it anyway.

Forgiving someone is not necessarily easy to do. We get that. But too many people get stuck on the "it's not fair" merry-go-round and fail to realize that forgiveness is an act of self-care.

Forgiveness is good for lots of reasons but chief among them is the fact that it benefits us as much, if not more, then the person we are forgiving. Not sure you are on board with that sentiment? Consider what Dr. Everett Worthington, researcher at Virginia Commonwealth University says (2020),

> Unforgiveness is stressful and holding unforgiving emotions and motives for long periods can take a toll on our bodies, leading to elevated blood pressure, heart rate, or cortisol. If those elevations persist, they can cause stress-related problems.

Holding on to resentment, anger, and grudges hurts. Literally. One of the kindest things you can do for yourself is to forgive others.

It is important to note that choosing to forgive someone does not mean that the other party should not be held accountable for their behavior. Nor does it mean that they'll avoid consequences. Forgiveness does not negate accountability. The point is that the person who benefits the most from forgiveness is the forgiver, not the forgiven. Remember, the other party may not deserve it, but you deserve to have the peace that comes with forgiveness.

When you find yourself struggling to forgive someone, consider this truth: you have been the beneficiary of undeserved grace and forgiveness. Setting aside the religious or faith-based connotations behind that statement, remember that lots of people have forgiven you for past offenses. You have offended and hurt people in your life. You have also been forgiven by many of those people. That forgiveness probably deepened relationships and helped lead to lasting change. So, if we have been forgiven by others, we should also seek to forgive.

But wait, we know it's not that easy. You may be thinking, "Yes, I have been forgiven. But I've never done anything as bad as what happened to me." That may be true. And if you are the victim of an abuse, we are not suggesting that you forgive to the extent that you open yourself up for repeated abuses. Rather, consider that forgiveness can offer you path forward. It offers *you* freedom.

In the book *The ABCs of Self-Care* (2022), author Sheri Betts reminds us of the risk of holding on to anger and resentment, "it's highly likely that the stress of unresolved anger, over time, can lead to issues far beyond those created by the original misconduct." She uses this analogy:

> Imagine everything you've ever owned (childhood toys, your first car, tax receipts, concert tickets from the early 1990s … everything) that you no longer have use for. Those things that don't interest you any longer or things that serve no good purpose in your current life. You have all of these things in a giant box sitting by your front door. Every time you leave the house, you have to take these things with you. They don't serve a good purpose anymore (although at one time they did) but they've lost their usefulness but you still carry them with you everywhere you go.

That's a bit of an over-the-top analogy, of course, but the idea is that we often carry with us hurts, offenses, and shame from the past that serve no good purpose in our current life. Some of us carry a "box" of negative emotions with us that unnecessarily weighs us down.

When it comes to forgiveness, we sometimes think, "OK, I'll forgive those people that ask for it. If they ask to be forgiven, I'll give it." There is a danger with this thinking. Aside from the fact that it is a bit egotistical, assumes your perspective or belief is 100% accurate, and makes you the final determiner of right and wrong (and your level of wisdom is probably not on par with Solomon), remember one important fact: *some people that have hurt you have no intention of making it right*. Did we just blow your mind on that one? Let's repeat it: *some people that have hurt you have no intention of making it right*. What a powerful statement! Other people may not care about mending the relationship or seeking forgiveness. And if we go even deeper along that line of thinking, consider another truth: *some people want you to stay hurt, offended, or mad*. It's their way of trying to control you. That why it is important to remember that forgiveness serves the forgiver more than the forgiven. Many of the people who have hurt you are either unaware of how deeply they've offended you, unconcerned with how deeply they've offended you, or both (Betts, 2022). Forgiveness is the first step in getting unstuck. We have to be open to forgiving both those who seek it but also to those who don't.

Not only do we practice forgiveness for stress management and resiliency-building, we also apologize when necessary. While our egos sometimes get in the way, offering a sincere apology to someone we have hurt or offended also provides a path forward. A heart-felt, genuine apology is freedom.

Our friend and colleague, Dr. Eric Jensen – author of dozens of books including the best-seller *Brain-Based Learning* (Jensen & McConchie, 2020) – notes that apologies are necessary for growth and change. He says, "You are powerless to fix what is invisible or denied." As leaders, we'll make mistakes. We need to own our mistakes and apologize when necessary. When you are tempted to hide, deny, or cover up a mistake, Dr. Jensen asks an important and insightful question, *"What are you really afraid of?"*

As leaders, our effectiveness is increased when we take ownership of mistakes. After all, everyone makes mistakes and no one expects you to be perfect. Now, let's go deeper and connect this idea (owning your mistakes and offering an apology) to the importance of expectations, patience, and grace granted to others. If you lead with such "high expectations" that you've created an atmosphere of fear and apprehension among your staff (that is, they are afraid of constant criticism), then when *you* make a mistake – and you will, lots of them – they'll want to crush you. If you don't grant grace to others when they mess up, when you mess up, they'll be quick to point out your hypocrisy.

A few last notes about offering an apology:

◆ Not every heartfelt apology will be accepted by the other party. But you do your part and let the other party deal with their own hang ups. If people hold a grudge, that says more about them than it does about you.
◆ When apologizing to someone, focus on what you did, not what the other party did. It's about you taking ownership, not trying to split the ownership.

- ◆ Never say, "I'm sorry you were offended" or "I'm sorry you feel that way." That's not an apology. It's a diversion.
- ◆ Avoid the use of "but." As you've likely heard many times, the use of "but" essentially negates the apology.
- ◆ As much as there really are legitimate times to blame, effective leaders tend to avoid it. Even when factors are outside your control, effective leaders understand that an apology is a path forward. In addition, when we blame others, it is essentially admitting that the other person has control over us.
- ◆ An apology followed by action shows true remorse. Say things like, "I'm sorry for my part in this. Here is what I am going to do to make things better."

Application Points

- ◆ *Remember* – Forgiving someone is simultaneously an act of courage, strength, and humility. The truly strong and secure offer forgiveness and deliver apologies. We are not suggesting that it is easy, we are proclaiming that it is worth it.
- ◆ *Reflect* – Ask questions, such as, "Who might I need to forgive?" and "Do I need to seek forgiveness from someone?" Also ask, "Do I need to forgive myself?"
- ◆ *Reflect some more* – Shame, embarrassment, and ego sometimes prevents us from offering or seeking forgiveness. When you find those emotions creeping up, consider how you'd respond to this statement, "I hid my mistake because ..." When we can come to grips with why we behave in certain ways, we can then take steps to improve in the future.
- ◆ *Put the ego in check* – Often, our ego is what stands in the way of giving or seeking forgiveness. And our ego is often wrapped up in how we think others view us (or how we believe they will view us in the future). As we work to establish an environment of grace, forgiveness, and second chances, the less our ego needs to be in charge.

◆ *Consider your mindset* – Carol Dweck, in her seminal 2006 book *Mindset* reminds us that forgiveness is a foundational practice for those with a growth mindset. When we hold on to grudges and offenses, it keeps us stuck in the past. Your life, your career, your relationships, and your ultimate purpose is in your future. Forgiving others is a way to move forward – for yourself and for others.

◆ *Analyze your self-talk* – When dealing with difficult situations, our internal dialogue can sometimes turn negative. Work to be aware of the way you describe, think about, and respond to conflict, difficult personalities, and change. Say things like, "I don't particularly want to forgive this person, but it is what is best. So, I forgive them for ..." Now might also be a good time to review the concepts and applications points from Chapter 13 (change) and Chapter 14 (conflict).

◆ *QTIP (quit taking it personally)* – We are convinced of this very important truth – much of our happiness is stolen by a pre-occupation with how other people behave. We mentioned it earlier – criticism comes with being a leader. Much of that criticism is unfounded. But if we go through life and career taking every offense (legitimate or not) personally, we'll be miserable.

◆ *But don't be callous* – The aim of QTIP is to put situations into perspective and not assume that everything is meant to be a personal offense. Quite simply – not everything is about you. Unless, of course, it is. It's a fine line we walk between being sensitive and overly sensitive. While we don't want to assume that everything is personal, we need to avoid extremes by assuming that nothing is.

◆ *Forgive as quickly as possible* – This is easier said than done. We get that. But there is no need to hang on to hurt longer than necessary.

◆ *Write it out* – To process forgiveness and to come to grips with any negative emotions, it may help to write statements such as "I forgive myself for..." or "I forgive _____ for..."

19

Resilient School Leaders – Tame ANTs

In a Nutshell

Automatic negative thoughts (ANTs) are intrusive, harmful thoughts and thinking patterns that impair our ability to think clearly during challenging times. Effective leaders recognize and combat ANTs in themselves and those they lead.

Digging Deeper

We all have them – strange, sometimes inappropriate, often negative intrusive thoughts that invade our thinking and thought patterns. Often happening at the most inconvenient of times, ANTs are reflections, ruminations, or notions that focus on the negative aspects of a situation. While we cannot always control what thoughts pop into our minds (or when), we can take specific actions to recognize thoughts that are harmful and take specific steps to tame them.

DOI: 10.4324/9781003301356-19

ANTs might include thoughts like:

◆ "Here we go again. I can't believe that person …!"
◆ "I'll never be able to …"
◆ "It is always going to be this way. I don't ever imagine it getting any better."
◆ "I'm such a screw up!"
◆ "I'm not smart enough to figure this out."
◆ "They obviously don't like me. So to heck with them!"
◆ "I'm an idiot for thinking I could do this."

Sometimes ANTs are focused on self; sometimes they are focused on others. But in all cases, the thinking pattern is negative and protective rather than hopeful or future oriented. It makes sense why we have ANTs – they serve to protect us from harm. They are also a bit of a cognitive shortcut that bypasses critical thinking (the slow, System 2 described in Chapter 11) in favor of a quick assessment and conclusion. In most cases the thoughts are self-defeating, often illogical, and almost always unhealthy in the long run.

ANTs are most often related to prior negative experiences or interactions with people. In some ways, they serve as defense mechanism in the brain. While that makes sense, not all of your brain's defense mechanisms are good for your long-term health and mental well-being.

Daniel and Tana Amen, in their 2016 book *The Brain Warrior's Way* remind us that we all have negative thoughts at times. It seems to simply be a byproduct of being a human being. Our brains do strange things at times; things that often don't make a lot of sense. But the Amens also remind us that just because we have a thought, doesn't make it true nor does it mean we have to entertain it. That bears repeating – just because a thought enters your mind, there is no rule that says it needs to stick around. In fact, entertaining and ruminating on those negative thoughts can be really harmful. And, the Amens are even more direct by stating, "Thoughts lie; they lie a lot, and it is our unquestioned or uninvestigated thoughts that steal our happiness. Having a thought has nothing to do with whether or not it is true." That is also worth repeating – *thoughts lie*. The existence of a thought does not make it true, right, or good.

Karen Reivich and Andrew Shattee, in their 2002 book *The Resilience Factor*, refer to ANTs as *intrusive thoughts*. We've all experienced moments where our minds wander to the negative, destructive, and sometimes morbid. They seem to sometimes just pop right out of the blue. According to Reivich and Shattee, intrusive thoughts undermine resilience because they focus on the negative, the catastrophic. And, by obsessing on problems we use mental and emotional resources that could be used for solving problems. And, quite simply, intrusive thoughts waste your time. So, they have some suggestions – simple ones that may seem a bit strange – but they work quite well. The next time you realize that ANTs or intrusive thoughts have taken over, try:

- ◆ The alphabet game – take a category (like types of fruit or first names) and start with the letter A and work through Z.
- ◆ Play categories – choose a category like famous novels or big cities and them name as many as you can.
- ◆ Rhyming – select a word and see how many others you can rhyme with it.
- ◆ Count – Start with 1000 and count backwards by 1s, 5s, 10s, etc.

These types of activities take mental, conscious effort. It will be nearly impossible to let ANTs run wild while doing one of these.

Dr. Tim Sharp (aka Dr. Happy) (2013) describes several categories of ANTs. Among the most significant, as they relate to stress management and resilience, are:

- ◆ *Overgeneralizing* – This is when we come to a broad, absolute conclusion based on limited experiences or interactions. If you find yourself in a negative state of mind about a person, ask yourself, "How often has this happened before?" If you cannot think of more than one or two examples, it may be an overgeneralization.

- *Filtering* – This is when we choose to focus only on the negative aspects of a situation while ignoring the positive. The truth is that everyone has something positive about them. This is true of people as well as organizations or groups. If you find yourself thinking something like "I know they said they would ____, but …," it's a good indication that you may be filtering. The use of "but," "however," or "although," is a dead-give away that you may be filtering.
- *All or nothing thinking* – This is exactly what it sounds like. Using phrases like "always" or "never" is a good indication that you may be falling into this trap. For example, if we think or say to ourselves, "That person never listens" we need to realize that it's not a true statement. It might feel like it, but it's not true that the person *never* listens.
- *Mindreading* – This is when we assume that we know what the other person is thinking. It's typically based on the conclusions we make about things like tone of voice, body posture, facial expressions, etc. It's dangerous and unhelpful to assume that you know what someone else is thinking.

You've likely already made this connection – ANTs are harmful for your relationships, your emotional well-being, your ability to lead others, and (this may be a surprise), your physical health (Marchant et al., 2020). Taming ANTs is really a method to manage emotional responses to a negative situation. Managing emotions is central to building resiliency (Gross & John, 2003). In fact, some researchers don't consider resiliency as a separate concept from emotional management; many simply refer to emotional resiliency.

Application Points

- *Reframe* – Simply talk to yourself differently. When we specifically choose a positive way to think about a negative situation, it changes perspective. Battling ANTs might start with a conscious effort to say something like,

"It looks and feels like _____ but I am going to think about it like _____."

◆ *Be mindful* – As we discussed in Chapter 6, mindfulness requires that we attend to the current moment in front of us. It requires that we pay specific attention to our mood, our mindsets, and our thinking patterns. When ANTs start to creep in, slow down and do your best to question them in a mindful way.

◆ *Teach staff and students about ANTs* – Specifically, help students to understand that, as Daniel and Tana Amen (2016) say, "Thoughts lie" and you don't have to entertain every thought that pops into your head.

◆ *Know your triggers* – A "trigger" is that thing (a person, an event, context, relationship) that knocks you back into a fixed mindset (Dweck, 2016). The triggering event essentially tells your brain to reject whatever is coming or to be on guard against a potential threat. Specifically, effective leaders know what behaviors among their staff, students, or parents may be a trigger for them. For example, as a reflective exercise, consider which of these behaviors are most likely pull you into a negative thinking pattern or assumption:
  • Lateness or tardiness to work or meetings.
  • Missing deadlines
  • Lack of empathy or grace to students, families, and co-workers
  • Lack of follow-through on commitments
  • Gossiping
  • Complaining
  • Calling in sick too often (missing work a lot)
  • Sarcasm
  • Negativity or bad attitudes
  • Reluctance to change or try new things
  • Saying, "Yeah, but ..."

◆ *Ask, "When do ANTs most likely appear?"* – For most of us, ANTs tend to show up when we are tired, overwhelmed, and stressed about our workload or schedule. Thus, the need to take care of yourself and "put your mask on first."

◆ *Label the emotion* – ANTs are essentially a way your brain tries to manage and channel negative emotions. Emotions, as you'll recall, cannot be controlled, but they can be managed. One simple way to begin is to label the emotion. Simply recognize the emotion and put words to it. Author of the book *Choke: What the Secrets of the Brain Reveal About getting it Right When You Have To* (2011), Sian Beilock, points out, there is power in simply recognizing that you are having an emotional response. Putting feelings into words helps to develop understanding and insight.

◆ *Label, then question* – It's OK to acknowledge a negative emotion or a negative thinking pattern. In fact, that's the first step – to label it. Acknowledge a less-than-productive thinking pattern and then ask yourself, "What do I need to do to change this pattern of thinking?" It's about taking action. Taking action and gaining control of your self-talk and internal dialogue can decrease stress.

◆ *Tell yourself, "It's not true"* – If you find yourself buying in and believing, even briefly, to your negative internal dialogue, you might simply try saying, "It feels like it's true, but this is a lie. It's not true. I know it's not true. I need to stop thinking like this." Remind yourself that feelings are not facts. Feelings and emotions are powerful, but they are not always accurate or true.

◆ *Have a "come to Jesus meeting" with yourself* – If you've never heard this phrase before, it refers to difficult discussions or interactions we have with people where we need to set the record straight. Most often we think of having these discussions with other people, particularly those we need to redirect or correct. During times of high stress when the ANTs are taking over, have one of these meetings with yourself. Ask yourself things like:

  • *"Am I always expecting things to be easy and to go my way?"*
  • *"Am I always expecting to get exactly what I want?"*
  • *"Am I feeling sorry for myself?"*

- *"Am I holding other people to a standard that is unrealistic?"*
- *"Am I holding on to a grudge?"*

◆ *Speaking of grudges* – Perhaps now is a good time to review what we discussed in Chapter 18 (forgive and apologize). When we forgive, it frees us up to move forward. Forgiveness is a good ANT repellant.

◆ *Remember that "thoughts lie"* – Shad Helmstetter, author of *Negative Self-Talk and How to Change it* (2019), reminds us of an important truth when battling ANTS, "What you believe about anything is not a measure of its correctness." What you believe about something is more a measure of your experiences, expectations, and biases.

◆ *Remember confirmation bias* – As we discussed in Chapter 14 (conflict), conformation bias is our brain's tendency to stick to a previously determined belief often to the extent of ignoring evidence that it may be wrong about something or someone. As we deal with our own ANTs, a simple strategy is to simply ask, "Could I be wrong about this?" Now, by the way, might be a good opportunity to review some of the concepts we discussed in the chapters on burnout, change, conflict, and dealing with difficult people. In all of those situations (dealing with difficult people, for example) ANTs are likely to appear.

20

Resilient School Leaders – Have Fun

In a Nutshell ✅

Amidst the challenges of work and leadership, intentionally addressing fun in the workplace is necessary for managing stress. Fun helps change your emotional state and strengthens motivation and productivity on the job. And, fun is well … fun. Everyone wants to work and learn in an environment of fun, joy, and energy.

Digging Deeper 🔍

School leaders deal with significant demands everyday – demands to increase test scores, to apply new initiatives or curriculum, to address the social-emotional needs of students and staff, etc. While we recognize that not everything in the workplace can be fun, it is important to create an atmosphere where laughter, fun, and enjoyment are a part of the culture.

You might find this interesting – did you know that fun, joy, and laughter have health benefits? Serious ones, in fact. According

DOI: 10.4324/9781003301356-20

to the Mayo Clinic (2021), laughter has both short-term and long-term benefits including the ability to decrease immediate stress and improve the body's long-term immune response. Fun activities release dopamine in the brain. Dopamine is an essential neurotransmitter that sends messages throughout the body. These messages are generally associated with attention, motivation, and reward. When things happen that are enjoyable and fun, chemicals in the brain are released and gives a feeling of pleasure. Even just the labeling of an activity as "fun" improves motivation and engagement (Hart & Albarracin, 2009). And, as you might have guessed, laughter and fun reduce stress (Berk, 2008).

Author and speaker Dr. Todd Whitaker, along with co-authors Beth Whitaker and Dale Lumpa, wrote in their highly-practical book titled *Motivating and Inspiring Teachers* (2013) that, it is our responsibility, as leaders, to meld the job so that it would be enjoyable to go to work each day. The fact is that we have a lot of control over how much fun we have at work. To manage stress better, find specific things that are fun and do them. As Dr. Whitaker suggests, approach each day with a "thank God it's Monday" attitude.

You may be asking yourself at this point, how do I create fun at work? One way is to start with your environment and school culture. Google (the company, not the verb) has a workplace culture that prioritizes fun. And Google is often at the top of lists of places with a positive workplace culture and happy employees. We certainly don't have the budget of a Fortune 500 company, but there are small things we can do to create a culture that priorities fun. For example, setting up a snack bar in the lounge for a fun break is simple, yet meaningful. You could also have fun themes such as "Orange you glad it's Friday" with orange items handed out to staff or "Two joke Tuesday" where everyone shares their favorite dad joke.

Dr. Allen Mendler, author of several books for educators (including co-authoring *Discipline with Dignity* with Richard Curwin) suggests that for optimal performance, we should have fun about 25% of our work time (2012). Now, that may or may not be realistic, but the idea is that fun and productivity are connected. Consider it a bit of a challenge to create opportunities for fun during the workday.

Application Points

- ◆ *Reflect on fun* – It's important to identify what "fun" is for you. Take the time to really consider what you enjoy, what makes you laugh, or what changes your mood for the better. When you figure it out, add those things to your day.
- ◆ *Make fun a priority* – As we discussed in Chapter 8 (organization), what gets scheduled, gets done! Spend the time building "fun" into your daily or weekly schedule. When things are scheduled, they tend to get done. Plus, when you tell other people about what you've scheduled, you are more likely to be accountable for it.
- ◆ *Tell a story* – Story telling is one way to make people laugh and have fun. It is a powerful way to immerse others in an experience and make connections. Whether you're laughing at yourself for something ridiculous you did, or sharing a funny story, laughter is a great way connect with others.
- ◆ *Create fun rituals* – Consider starting off every staff or team meeting with a joke of the day. It will become contagious and people will look forward to the start of your meetings. Can you imagine that – staff who eagerly look forward to you starting a staff meeting?
- ◆ *Hold a pop-up event* – Announcing that there will be special "pop-up" days where staff and students get to do something fun (wearing silly socks, for example) can help to create a fun work atmosphere.
- ◆ *Take pictures* – When students and staff are having fun, take pictures and share them with staff, students, and families
- ◆ *Change the meeting* – Instead of holding a staff meeting inside, hold it outside or in a different location where there are fun props or games. Embedding language or

activities from shows such as *Survivor* or *Name That Tune* is a fun way to connect the content to fun.

◆ *Ask your staff* – We've already noted that not everything at school can be fun. We get that. But a good place to start is by simply asking staff, "What can we do to make the environment more enjoyable?"

◆ *Remember that sarcasm hurts* – It probably does not need to be said, but we'll say it anyway. Sarcasm is a no-no. It has no place in our leadership toolbox. While it is a form of humor, it's not an appropriate one for a school leader.

Bibliography

Achor, S. (2010). *The Happiness Advantage*. Crown Business.

Aguilar, E. (2018). *Onward: Cultivating Emotional Resilience in Educators*. Jossey-Bass.

Allen, S. (2018). *The Science of Gratitude*. John Templeton Foundation.

Amason, A., Mooney, A., &. Holahan, P. (2007). Don't take it personally: Exploring cognitive conflict as a mediator of affective conflict. *Journal of Management Studies*, 44(5): 733–758. https://doi.org/10.1111/j.1467-6486.2006.00674.x

Amen, D. & Amen, T. (2016). *The Brain Warriors Way*. New American Library.

Amen, D. (2022). *You, Happier*. Tyndale.

American Psychological Association. (2020, April). Nurtured by nature. *Monitor on Psychology*, 51(3). www.apa.org/monitor/2020/04/nurtured-nature

Barnes, A. (2021). *How to De-Stress*. Circus Books.

Beilock, S. (2011). *Choke: What the Secrets of the Brain Reveal about Getting It Right When You Have To*. Atria Press.

Berk, L. (2008). Anticipating a laugh reduces our stress hormones, study shows. *ScienceDaily*. www.sciencedaily.com/releases/2008/04/080407114617.htm

Betts, S. (2022). *The ABCs of Self-Care*. Balboa Press.

Birnie, K., Speca, M., & Carlson, L.E. (2010). Exploring self-compassion and empathy in the context of mindfulness-based stress reduction (MBSR). *Stress and Health*, 26: 359–371. https://doi.org/10.1002/smi.1305

Boggiss, A.L., Consedine, N.S., Brenton-Peters, J.M., Hofman, P.L., & Serlachius, A.S. (2020). A systematic review of gratitude interventions: Effects on physical health and health behaviors. *Journal of Psychosomatic Research,* 135: 110165.

Bourassa, K.J., Ruiz, J.M., & Sbarra, D.A. (2019). The impact of physical proximity and attachment working models on cardiovascular reactivity: Comparing mental activation and romantic partner presence. *Psychophysiology*, 56: e13324. https://doi.org/10.1111/psyp.13324

Bremner, J.D., Moazzami, K., Wittbrodt, M.T., Nye, J.A., Lima, B.B., Gillespie, C.F., Rapaport, M.H., Pearce, B.D., Shah, A.J., & Vaccarino, V. (2020). Diet, stress and mental health. *Nutrients*, 2020; 12(8): 2428. https://doi.org/10.3390/nu12082428

Buck, F. (2018). In Pursuit of a Balanced Life. AMLE Magazine, 6(1). www.amle.org/in-pursuit-of-the-balanced-life/

Burzynska, A.Z., Wong, C.N., Voss, M.W., Cooke, G.E., Gothe, N.P., Fanning, J., et al. (2015). Physical activity is linked to greater moment-to-moment variability in spontaneous brain activity in older adults. *PLoS ONE* 10(8): e0134819. https://doi.org/10.1371/journal.pone.0134819

Chae, B., & Zhu, R. (2014). Environmental disorder leads to self-regulatory failure. *Journal of Consumer Research*, 40(6): 1203–1218.

Chamorro-Premuzic, T. (2021). Just hire better bosses. In *HBR Guide to Beating Burnout*. Harvard Business Review Press.

Coleman, J. (2018). You don't find your purpose, you build it. *Harvard Business Review*. https://hbr.org/2017/10/you-dont-find-your-purpose-you-build-it

Comer, J. (2019). *The Ruthless Elimination of Hurry*. WaterBrook.

Couros, G. (2020). Change is an opportunity to do something amazing. https://georgecouros.ca/blog/archives/5352

Covey, S. (2013). *The 7 Habits of Highly Effective People*. Simon and Schuster.

Crum, A.J., Salovey, P., & Achor, S. (2013). Rethinking stress: The role of mindsets in determining the stress response. *Journal of Personality and Social Psychology*, 104(4), 716–733. https://doi.org/10.1037/a0031201

Darmody, M., & Smyth, E. (2011). *Job Satisfaction and Occupational Stress among Primary School Teachers and School Principals in Ireland*. ESRI.

David, S. & Congleton, C. (2013). Emotional agility. https://hbr.org/2013/11/emotional-agility

Davidson, R. (2012). *The Emotional Life of Your Brain: How Its Unique Patterns Affect the Way You Think, Feel, and Live – and How You Can Change Them*. Avery.

De Jong, D., Grundmeyer, T., & Yankey, J. (2017) Identifying and addressing themes of job dissatisfaction for secondary principals. *School Leadership & Management*, 37(4): 354–371. DOI: 10.1080/13632434.2017.1338253

DeMatthews, D., Carrola, P., Reyes, P., & Knight, D. (2021). School leadership burnout and job-related stress: Recommendations for district administrators and principals. *The Clearing House: A Journal of Educational Strategies, Issues and Ideas*, 94(4): 159–167, DOI: 10.1080/00098655.2021.1894083

DePree, M. (2004). *Leadership Is an Art*. Currency Doubleday.

Dobson, P. (2016). *The Brain Book*. LID Publishing.

D'Sousa, S. (2021). Don't get surprised by burnout. *In HBR Guide to Beating Burnout*. Harvard Business Review Press.

Duckworth, A. (2016). *Grit: The Power of Passion and Perseverance*. Scribner.

Dweck, C. (2006). *Mindset*. Robinson.

Dweck, C. (2016). "Carol Dweck revisits the growth mindset". *Education Week*, 35(5): 20–24.

Emmons, R.A., & McCullough, M.E. (2003). Counting blessings versus burdens: An experimental investigation of gratitude and subjective well-being in daily life. *Journal of Personality and Social Psychology*, 84(2): 377–389. https://doi.org/10.1037/0022-3514.84.2.377

Emo Philips Quotes. (n.d.). BrainyQuote.com. Retrieved October 11, 2022, from: www.brainyquote.com/quotes/emo_philips_128947.

Eurich, T. (2018). What self-awareness really is (and how to cultivate it). *Harvard Business Review*, 1–9.

Fabritius, F. & Hageman, H. (2017). *The Leading Brain*. Tarcher Perigree.

Farber, S. (2004). *The Radical Leap*. Dearborn.

Ferriss, T. (2009). *The 4-Hour Workweek*. Crown Publishers.

Fishman, M.D. (2020). The silver linings journal: Gratitude during a pandemic. *Journal of Radiology Nursing*, 39(3): 149.

Flaherty, J. (2005). *Coaching: Evoking Excellent in Others*. Elsevier Press.

Fowler, J. & Christakis, N. (2011). *Connected: The Surprising Power of Our Social Networks and How They Shape Our Lives*. Little Brown Spark.

Frey, N., Fisher, D., & Pumpian, I. (2012). *How to Create a Culture of Achievement*. ASCD.

Fullan, M. (2008). *The Six Secrets of Change*. Josey Bass.

Gardener, H. et al. (2016). Ideal cardiovascular health and cognitive aging in the Northern Manhattan study. *Journal of the American Heart Association*, 5: e002731.

Ghannoum, M., Ford, M., Bonomo, R.A., Gamal, A., McCormick, T.S. (2021). A Microbiome-driven approach to combating depression during the COVID-19 pandemic. *Front Nutr.*, 8: 672390. doi: 10.3389/fnut.2021.672390. PMID: 34504858; PMCID: PMC8421528.

Green, R. (2009). *Practicing the Art of Leadership*. Allyn & Bacon.

Greenleaf, R. (1977). *Servant Leadership*. Paulist Press.

Gross, J., & John, O. (2003). Individual differences in two emotion regulation processes: Implications for affect, relationships, and well being. *Journal of Personality and Social Psychology*, 85: 348–362.

Haghighatdoost, F., Feizi, A., Esmaillzadeh, A., Rashidi-Pourfard, N., Keshteli, A.H., Roohafza, H., Adibi, P. (2018). Drinking plain water is associated with decreased risk of depression and anxiety in adults: Results from a large cross-sectional study. *World J Psychiatry*. Sep 20; 8(3): 88–96. doi: 10.5498/wjp.v8.i3.88. PMID: 30254979; PMCID: PMC6147771.

Hanson, R. (2018). *Resilient: How to Grown an Unshakeable Core of Calm, Strength, and Happiness*. Harmony Books.

Hanson, R., & Hanson, F. (2020). *Resilient: How to Grow an Unshakable Core of Calm, Strength, and Happiness*. Harmony Books.

Harris, B. (2021). *17 Things Resilient Teachers Do (and 4 Things They Hardly Ever Do)*. Routledge.

Hart, W., & Albarracín, D. (2009). The effects of chronic achievement motivation and achievement primes on the activation of achievement and fun goals. *Journal of Personality and Social Psychology*, 97(6): 1129.

Hecht, E., Rabil, A., Martinez Steele, E., Abrams, G., Ware, D., Landy, D., & Hennekens, C. (2022). Cross-sectional examination of ultra-processed food consumption and adverse mental health symptoms. *Public Health Nutrition*, 1–10. doi:10.1017/S1368980022001586

Hedges, K. (2018). Five questions to help your employees find their inner purpose. *Harvard Business Review*. https://hbr.org/2017/08/5-questions-to-help-your-employees-find-their-inner-purpose

Helmstetter, S. (2019). *Negative Self-Talk and How to Change It*. Park Avenue Press.

Henderson, N., & Milstein, M.M. (2003). *Resiliency in Schools: Making It Happen for Students and Educators*. Corwin Press.

Hill, P.L., & Turiano, N.A. (2014). Purpose in life as a predictor of mortality across adulthood. *Psychol Sci*. Jul; 25(7):1482–1486. doi:10.1177/0956797614531799. Epub 2014 May 8. PMID:24815612; PMCID: PMC4224996.

Hirotsu, C., Tufik, S., & Andersen, M.L. (2015). Interactions between sleep, stress, and metabolism: From physiological to pathological conditions. *Sleep Sci.* Nov; 8(3): 143–152. doi: 10.1016/j.slsci.2015.09.002. Epub 2015 Sep 28. PMID: 26779321; PMCID: PMC 4688585.

Holt-Lunstad, J., Smith, T.B., & Layton, J.B. (2010). Social relationships and mortality risk: a meta-analytic review. *PLoS Med.*, 7(7): e1000316. doi: 10.1371/journal.pmed.1000316. PMID: 20668659; PMCID: PMC 2910600.

Howard, P. (2006). *The Owner's Manual for the Brain.* Bard Press.

Jensen, E. (2005). *Teaching with the Brain in Mind.* ASCD.

Jensen, E., & McConchie, L. (2020). *Brain-based Learning: Teaching the Way Students Really Learn.* Corwin.

John Templeton Foundation. (n.d.). Research on Forgiveness. Retrieved October 11, 2022, from www.templeton.org/discoveries/forgiveness

Johnson, S. (1999). *Who Moved my Cheese?* Vermillion.

Jones, P. (2017). *Exactly What to Say: The Magic Words for Influence and Impact.* Box of Tricks Publishing.

Kahneman, D. (2013). *Thinking, Fast and Slow.* Farrar, Straus and Giroux.

Keng, S.L., Smoski, M.J., Robins, C.J. (2011). Effects of mindfulness on psychological health: A review of empirical studies. *Clin Psychol Rev.* Aug; 31(6): 1041–1056. doi: 10.1016/j.cpr.2011.04.006. Epub 2011 May 13. PMID: 21802619; PMCID: PMC3679190.

Kennedy, S. & Mitchell, L. (2019). *Restore: 20 Self-Care Rituals to Reclaim Your Energy.* Hinkler.

Kong, F., Zhao, J., You, X., & Xiang, Y. (2020). Gratitude and the brain: Trait gratitude mediates the association between structural variations in the medial prefrontal cortex and life satisfaction. *Emotion*, 20(6): 917.

Kouzes, J. and Posner, B. (1987). *The Leadership Challenge.* Jossey-Bass.

Leanse, E. (2017). *The Happiness Hack.* Simple Truths.

Levitin, D. (2020). *Successful Aging.* Dutton.

Liska, D., Mah, E., Brisbois, T., Barrios, P.L., Baker, L.B., & Spriet, L.L. (2019). Narrative review of hydration and selected health outcomes in the general population. *Nutrients*, Jan 1; 11(1): 70. doi: 10.3390/nu11010070. PMID: 30609670; PMCID: PMC6356561.

Mahatma Gandhi Quotes. (n.d.). BrainyQuote.com. Retrieved October 11, 2022, from: www.brainyquote.com/quotes/mahatma_gandhi_121411.

Mansfield, C., Beltman, S., & Price, A. (2014). 'I'm coming back again!' The resilience process of early career teachers. *Teachers and Teaching*, 20: 1–21. 10.1080/13540602.2014.937958.

Marchant, N.L., Lovland, L.R., Jones, R., et al. (2020). Repetitive negative thinking is associated with amyloid, tau, and cognitive decline. *Alzheimer's Dement*, 16: 1054–1064. https://doi.org/10.1002/alz.12116

Margolis, J. & Stoltz, P. (2018). How to bounce back from adversity. *Harvard Business Review*. https://hbr.org/2010/01/how-to-bounce-back-from-adversity

Maslach, C. & Leiter, M.P. (2016). Understanding the burnout experience: recent research and its implications for psychiatry. *World Psychiatry*, 15(2): 103–111. doi: 10.1002/wps.20311. PMID: 27265691; PMCID: PMC4911781.

Mayo Clinic (2017). Depressions and anxiety: Exercise eases symptoms. www.mayoclinic.org/diseases-conditions/depression/in-depth/depression-and-exercise/art-20046495

Mayo Clinic (2021). Stress relief from laughter? It's no joke. www.mayoclinic.org/healthy-lifestyle/stress-management/in-depth/stress-relief/art-20044456

McGregor, H.A., & Elliot, A.J. (2005). The shame of failure: Examining the link between fear of failure and shame. *Personality and Social Psychology Bulletin*, *31*(2): 218–231.

McKee, A. & Wiens, K. (2021). Making compassion a habit. In *HBR Guide to Beating Burnout*. Harvard Business Review Press.

Medina, J. (2008). *Brain Rules*. Pear Press.

Mendler, A. (2012). *When Teaching Gets Tough: Smart Ways to Reclaim your Game*. ASCD.

Mendler, A. (2014). *The Resilient Teacher*. ASCD.

Mendler, A.N. (2021). *Motivating Students Who Don't Care: Proven Strategies to Engage All Learners*. Solution Tree.

Mintzberg, H. (2005). *Managers Not MBAs: A Hard Look at the Soft Practice of Managing and Management Development*. Berrett-Koehler Publishers.

Moss, J. (2020). Rethinking burnout: When self care is not the cure. *American Journal of Health Promotion.* 34(5): 565–568. doi:10.1177/0890117120920488b

Mullen, C.A., Shields, L.B., & Tienken, C.H. (2021). Developing teacher resilience and resilient school cultures. *Journal of Scholarship & Practice,* 18(1): 8–24.

Nestor, J. (2020). *Breath: The New Science of a Lost Art.* Riverhead Books.

Oaklander, M. (2015). *The Science of Bouncing Back.* Time. https://time.com/3892044/the-science-of-bouncing-back/

Oberle, E. & Schonert-Reichl, K. (2016). Stress contagion in the classroom? The link between classroom teacher burnout and morning cortisol in elementary school students. *Social Science & Medicine,* 159. 10.1016/j.socscimed.2016.04.031.

Ohrnberger, J., Fichera, E., & Sutton, M. (2017). The relationship between physical and mental health: A mediation analysis. *Soc Sci Med,* Dec; 195: 42–49. doi: 10.1016/j.socscimed.2017.11.008. Epub 2017 Nov 8. PMID: 29132081.

Pargament, K.I. (1997). *The Psychology of Religion and Coping: Theory, Research, Practice.* The Guilford Press.

Park, S., Kahnt, T., Dogan, A. et al. (2017). A neural link between generosity and happiness. *Nat Commun,* 8: 15964. https://doi.org/10.1038/ncomms15964

Patterson, J. & Kelleher, P. (2005). *Resilient School Leaders.* ASCD.

Pellicer, L. (2008). *Caring Enough to Lead.* Corwin Press.

Reivich, K. & Shattee, A. (2002). *The Resilience Factor.* Broadway Books.

Robinson, N. (2018). *Looming Crisis in School Leadership: One in Five Principals Is Burnt Out.* ABC Education.

Sander, L. (2019). The case for finally cleaning your desk. https://hbr.org/2019/03/the-case-for-finally-cleaning-your-desk

Sander, E.J., Caza, A., & Jordan, P.J. (2019). Psychological perceptions matter: Developing the reactions to the physical work environment scale, *Building and Environment,* 148: 338–347, ISSN 0360-1323, https://doi.org/10.1016/j.buildenv.2018.11.020.

Sapolsky, R. (2004). *Why Zebras Don't Get Ulcers.* St Martin's Griffen.

Segerstrom, S.C., & Miller, G.E. (2004). Psychological stress and the human immune system: a meta-analytic study of 30 years of inquiry. *Psychol Bull,* 130(4): 601–630. doi: 10.1037/0033-2909.130.4.601. PMID: 15250815; PMCID: PMC1361287.

Seligman, M. (2006). *Learned Optimism*. Vintage Books

Seppala, E. (2020). The secrets of a happier life in the science of happiness. *Time Magazine Special Edition*.

Sharp, T. (2013). Examples of Automatic Negative Thoughts (ANTS). The Positive Times, https://positivetimes.com.au/examples-of-automatic-negative-thoughts-ants-by-tim-sharp-dr-happy/

Shoho, A.R., & Barnett, B.G. (2010). The realities of new principals: Challenges, joys, and sorrows. *Journal of School Leadership*, 20(5): 561–596. https://doi.org/10.1177/105268461002000503

Siegel, D. (2007). *The Mindful Brain*. W.W. Norton & Company.

Sinek, S. (2011). *Start With Why*. Penguin.

Skaalvik, E.M., & Skaalvik, S. (2021). Teacher stress and coping strategies: The struggle to stay in control. *Creative Education*, 12(6): 1273–1295.

Skovholt, T. & Trotter-Mathison, M. (2016). *The Resilient Practitioner: Burnout and Compassion Fatigue Prevention and Self-Care Strategies for the Helping Professions*. Routledge.

Solms, M. (2021). *The Hidden Spring*. Norton Press.

Southwick, F.S., Martini, B.L., Charney, D.S., & Southwick, S.M. (2017). Leadership and resilience. In *Leadership today* (pp. 315–333). Springer.

Southwick, S.M., & Charney, D.S. (2018). *Resilience: The Science of Mastering Life's Greatest Challenges*. Cambridge University Press.

Steiger A, Pawlowski M. (2019). Depression and sleep. *International Journal of Molecular Sciences*, 20(3): 607. https://doi.org/10.3390/ijms20030607

Steiner, E. et al. (2022). *Restoring Teacher and Principal Well-Being Is an Essential Step for Rebuilding Schools: Findings from the State of the American Teacher and State of the American Principal Surveys*. RAND Corporation. www.rand.org/pubs/research_reports/RRA1108-4.html.

Superville, D. (2018). 'I want a job and a life': How principals find balance in all-consuming work. EducationWeek. www.edweek.org/leadership/i-want-a-job-and-a-life-how-principals-find-balance-in-all-consuming-work/2018/10

Sutton, R. (2007). *The No Asshole Rule: Building a Civilized Workplace and Surviving One That Isn't*. Warner Business Books.

Sutton, R. (2012). *Good Boss, Bad Boss: How to Be the Best... and Learn from the Worst*. Business Plus.

Thrall, B., McNicol, B. & McElrath, K. (1999). *The Ascent of a Leader.* Jossey-Bass.

Tyler Perry Quotes. (n.d.). BrainyQuote.com. Retrieved October 11, 2022, from: www.brainyquote.com/quotes/tyler_perry_418193

Upadyaya, K., Toyama, H., & Salmela-Aro, K. (2021). School principals' stress profiles during COVID-19, demands, and resources. *Front Psychol.,* 12: 731929. doi: 10.3389/fpsyg.2021.731929. PMID: 34975620; PMCID: PMC8716552.

Werner, E.E., & Smith, R.S. (1992). *Overcoming the Odds: High Risk Children from Birth to Adulthood.* Cornell University Press.

Whiteside, D. (2018). *The Anatomy of a Purpose-Driven Employee.* www.davewhiteside.com/anatomyofapurposedrivenemployee

Wigert, B., & Agrawal, S. (2018). Employee Burnout, Part 1: The 5 Main Causes. Gallup www.gallup.com/workplace/237059/employee-burnout-part-main-causes.aspx

Wisse, B., & Sleebos, E. (2016). When change causes stress: Effects of self-construal and change consequences. *Journal of Business and Psychology,* 31: 249–264. https://doi.org/10.1007/s10869-015-9411-z

Whitaker, T., Whitaker, B., & Lumpa, D. (2008). *Motivating and Inspiring Teachers: Eye On Education.* Routledge.

Whitaker, T., Whitaker, B., & Lumpa, D. (2013). *Motivating & Inspiring Teachers: The Educational Leader's Guide for Building Staff Morale.* Routledge.

Wolin, S., & Wolin, S.J. (1996). The challenge model: Working with strengths in children of substance-abusing parents. *Child and Adolescent Psychiatric Clinics of North America,* **5**(1), 243–256.

Yano, J.M., Yu, K., Donaldson, G.P., Shastri, G.G., Ann, P., Ma, L., Nagler, C.R., Ismagilov, R.F., Mazmanian, S.K., & Hsiao, E,Y. (2015). Indigenous bacteria from the gut microbiota regulate host serotonin biosynthesis. *Cell,* 161(2): 264–276. ISSN 0092-8674. PMCID PMC4393509. https://resolver.caltech.edu/CaltechAUTHORS:20150409-093248232

Zelman, K.M. (2008). The wonders of water. WebMD. www.webmd.com/a-to-z-guides/features/wonders-of-water

Ziglar, Z. (1975). *See You at the Top.* We Believe Inc.

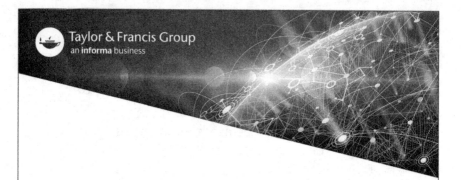

Printed in the United States
by Baker & Taylor Publisher Services